Christ Our Righteousness

Jesus is going from door to door, standing in front of every soul-temple, proclaiming, 'I stand at the door, and knock.' As a heavenly merchantman, He opens His treasures, and cries, 'Buy of Me gold tried in the fire, that thou mayest be rich; and white raiment, that thou mayest be clothed, and that the shame of thy nakedness do not appear.' . . . Open your doors, says the great merchantman, the possessor of spiritual riches, and transact your business with Me. It is I, your Redeemer, who counsels you to buy of Me."—Mrs. E. G. White.

The Waiting One

(This poem appeared in the *Review and Herald* of July 31, 1888, the year in which the message of "Righteousness by Faith" came so clearly and decidedly to God's people. The spirit of that solemn message evidently called forth these beautiful stanzas.)

"'BEHOLD, I stand at the door, and knock!'
   Hearest thou, Heart, that voice most sweet?
Wilt thou not up and undo the lock
   And make a space for His holy feet?
What? Thou art weary and sick with woe,
And wilt not arise for the Stranger so?

"But, Heart, He's the Great Physician, true.
   He beareth a cordial for every smart.
And ah! He has come for His pity of you.
   Rouse thee a moment, my poor, faint heart.
Let thee die? O Heart! Canst thou say it o'er
When the Great Physician is at the door?

"Listen, my Heart. Do you hear Him weep?
   Oh! His soul is exceedingly grieved for thee.
He has forded the rivers so wide and deep.
   And the dangers about Him were sore to see.
And, O my Heart! His dear hands and brow
Are blood-stained, and wounded, and bleeding now.

"What? Wilt thou not believe it, Heart?
   Sayest thou none ever cared for thee?
Oh! Whisper it low, for no crueler dart
   Could so pierce to His tender soul, I see.
Oh! Could I but tell thee what grief befell.
For the love that he bore thee, unutterable.

The Waiting One

"Let Him in, my Heart, let me still persuade;
  He will robe thee in beauty like His, divine.
He will free thee out of this prison's shade.
  And take thee into His courts to shine.
Leaning on Him, thy Beloved, thou'lt go
To His gardens of spice, where the lilies grow.

"Slowly my Heart to the door has crept,
  Her weak hand pushes aside the lock.
She looks in the eyes that for her have wept,
  And kisses the hands that so long did knock.
She weeps at His feet till her soul is mild,
And she clings to Him now, like a trusting child.

"Oh, how He loves her! How sweet the tryst!
  Her sickness is over, her robe is white.
She findeth her all in all in Christ,
  And her prison is flooded with holy light,
And she sits at the board, and she sups His wine,
And feasts in the love of her Lord divine.

"'Oh! How could I leave Thee outside so long?'
  She weeps as she thinks of his tender love;
But He freely forgives her bitter wrong.
  And makes her to be a partaker of
His own sweet nature, and seals her His
By many a pledge of deep tenderness."

Christ Our Righteousness

A study of the Principles of Righteousness
by Faith as Set Forth in the Word of God and
the Writings of the Spirit of Prophecy

By

ARTHUR G. DANIELLS

ISBN-13: 978-1494730314

ISBN: 1494730316

The content has been edited in minor ways for the convenience of the reader. The layout has changed and the spelling of specific words have been modified. All else is meant to be identical to the edition printed in 1926.

Textual and Topical Indices have also been added to the end of the content.

Contents

Part I—The Enunciation in Scripture   **Page**

1. Christ Our Righteousness.............................15

Part II—The Witness of the Spirit of Prophecy

2. A Message of Supreme Importance 27

3. Preparatory Messages.................................31

4. The Message Set Forth at the
   Minneapolis Conference 42

5. A New Era in the Proclamation of the
   Third Angel's Message 53

6. The Third Angel's Message in Verity.....................59

Part III—A Study of the Scope of the Subject

7. A Fundamental, All-Embracing Truth..................67

8. The Deadly Peril of Formalism...........................71

9. The Great Truth Lost Sight Of 79

10. Restoration Full and Complete Provided.............85

11. Entering Into the Experience 92

Appendix...99

Textual Index.. 132

Topical Index.. 134

FORWARD

At a meeting of the members of the Ministerial Association Advisory Council, held in Des Moines, Iowa, Oct. 22, 1924, it was—

"*Voted,* That Elder Daniells be asked to arrange for a compilation of the writings of Mrs. E. G. White on the subject of Justification by Faith."

This official request voiced a desire that had long been felt and often expressed by many of our workers and people, entire union conferences having gone on record as requesting such a production. With the co-operation of my associates in the office of the Ministerial Association, I undertook the task designated.

In harmony with the primary purpose of providing a "compilation of the writings of Mrs. E. G. White on the subject," exhaustive research was made through all the writings of the spirit of prophecy as held in trust by us as a people, in bound volumes and also in printed articles appearing in the files of our denominational papers, covering a period of twenty-five year from 1887-1912. So vast was the field of study opened up, so marvelous and illuminating the hidden gems of truth which came to light, that I became amazed and awed at the solemn obligation resting upon me, of rescuing these gems from their obscurity, and placing them, in a cluster of brilliancy and beauty, where they would win rightful recognition and acceptance in the glorious finishing of the work intrusted to the remnant church.

Seeking advice and counsel from my colleagues, I sent out advance sections of the manuscript for careful reading and suggestion. The response from fellow laborers in all sections of the North American field has been a most encouraging and appreciative nature, and urgency in completing the work has been emphasized. A suggestion made by a number of fellow ministers has led to the preparation of a chapter on the subject of righteousness by faith from the Bible standpoint as an introduction to the compilation from the writings of the spirit of prophecy. This, it is believed, will give Scriptural authority and permanence to the theme which is of such vital importance to God's people at this time.

The Word of God clearly portrays the way of righteousness by faith; the writings of the spirit of prophecy greatly amplify and elucidate the subject. In our blindness and dullness of heart, we have wandered far out of the way, and for many years have been failing to appropriate this sublime truth. But all the while our great Leader has been calling His people to come into line on this great fundamental of the gospel,-- receiving by faith the *imputed* righteousness of Christ for sins that are past, and the *imparted* righteousness of Christ for revealing the divine nature in human flesh.

In order to make this compilation of the greatest value, it seemed necessary to do more than merely bring together a long series of miscellaneous, detached statements. Appropriate arrangement and combination were necessary, and the chronological order was important: also, the circumstances and issues concerning which particular statements were made, should be rightly understood. Unless these considerations were recognized, the compilation might prove confusing and wearisome.

A careful, connected study of the writings of the spirit of prophecy regarding the subject of righteousness by faith, has led to the settled conviction that the instruction given presents two aspects: primarily, the great, amazing fact that by faith in the Son of God, sinners may receive the righteousness of God: and secondarily, the purpose and providence of God in sending the specific message of receiving the righteousness of God by faith to His people assembled in General Conference in the city of Minneapolis, Minnesota, in the year 1888. This latter aspect cannot be disregarded by Seventh-day Adventists without missing a most important lesson that the Lord designed to teach us. It is this conviction that has made it seem necessary to include in the compilation the instruction given concerning the experiences and developments connected with and following the Minneapolis Conference.

The major portion of our membership today has been raised up since these experiences came to us. They are unacquainted with them; but they read the message; also the lessons which those experiences were designed to teach. Hence the necessity of reproducing a portion, at least, of the instruction then given, and accompanying the same with a brief explanation of what took place.

Those who have full confidence in the gift of the spirit of prophecy, to the remnant church will place great value upon the compilation of statements herein furnished. Only a few of them have ever been reproduced since they first appeared in the columns of the *Review and Herald.* Most of them dropped out of sight with the current number of the *Review* in which they appeared. In no other document have all of these been brought together in systematic and chronological form, as here presented. May those messages do their appointed work in the lives of all who read these pages. Wondrous is the blessing Heaven is waiting to bestow!

A.G.D.

"CLAD IN THE ARMOR OF CHRIST'S RIGHTEOUSNESS. THE CHURCH IS TO ENTER UPON HER FINAL CONFLICT."

Mrs. E. G. White.

"ON CHRIST'S CORONATION DAY HE WILL NOT ACKNOWLEDGE AS HIS ANY WHO BEAR SPOT OR WRINKLE OR ANY SUCH THING. BUT TO HIS FAITHFUL ONES HE WILL GIVE CROWNS OF IM-MORTAL GLORY. THOSE WHO WOULD NOT THAT HE SHOULD REIGN OVER THEM WILL SEE HIM SURROUNDED BY THE ARMY OF THE REDEEMED. EACH OF WHOM BEARS THE SIGN. THE LORD OUR RIGHTEOUSNESS."

Mrs. E. G. White.

PART I

The Enunciation in Scripture

"The righteous Lord loveth righteousness" Ps. 11:7.

"There is not unrighteousness in Him. Ps. 92:15.

"Awake to righteousness and sin not." 1 Cor. 15:34.

Chapter One

Christ Our Righteousness

C hrist our righteousness is the one sublime message set forth in the Sacred Scriptures. However varied the forms and phrases in which this message ay be unfolded and presented, yet always, from every point of the circle, the central commanding theme is, Christ our righteousness.

The account of creation reveals the marvelous wisdom and power of Christ, by whom all things were created. Col. 1:14-16. The sin of the first Adam, with all its awful consequences, is related in order that Christ, the last Adam, may be hailed as Redeemer and restorer. Rom. 5:12-21. Death with all its terrors is set before us, that Christ may be exalted and glorified as the Life-giver. 1 Cor. 15:22. The disappointments, sorrows, and tragedies of this life are recounted, that Christ may be sought as the great comforter and deliverer. John 16:33. Our sinful, corrupt natures are presented in lurid colors, that Christ may be appealed to for cleansing, and may in very deed be unto us "the Lord our righteousness."

Thus it is throughout the Sacred Volume,—every phase of truth unfolded, points in some way to Christ as our righteousness.

But righteousness as a distinct, well-defined subject of vital importance, occupies a large place in the Word of God. Its source, its nature, the possibility of its being obtained by sinners, and the conditions upon which it may be secured, are set forth in great clearness in that original authoritative textbook on righteousness.

Of the *source* of righteousness, we read: "O Lord, righteousness belongeth unto Thee." Dan. 9:7. "The Lord is righteous in all His ways." Ps. 145:17. "Thy righteousness is like the great mountains." Ps. 36:6. "Thy righteousness is an everlasting righteousness." Ps. 119:142. "The righteous Lord loveth righteousness." Ps. 11:7. "There is no unrighteousness in Him." Ps. 92:15.

Regarding the *nature* of righteousness, the Scriptures are most explicit. It is set forth as the very opposite of sin, and is associated with holiness, or godliness. "Awake to righteousness, and sin not." 1 Cor. 15:34. "That ye put away, as concerning your former manner of life, the old man, which waxeth corrupt after the lusts of deceit; and that ye be renewed in the spirit of your mind, and put on the new man, which after God hath been created in righteousness and holiness of truth." Eph. 4:22-24, R.V. "The fruit of the Spirit is in all goodness and righteousness and truth." Eph. 5:9. "Follow after righteousness, godliness, faith, love, patience, meekness." 1 Tim. 6:11. "All unrighteousness is sin." 1 John 5:17.

Perhaps the finest and most inspiring statement regarding the righteousness in all the Word of God is the following concerning Christ: "Thou has loved righteousness, and hated iniquity; therefore God, even Thy God, hath anointed Thee with the oil of gladness above Thy fellows." Heb. 1:9. This places righteousness as the antithesis, the direct opposite, of iniquity or sin.

Thus the Word declares that God is the source of righteousness, and that it is one of His divine, holy attributes.

The supreme question regarding the righteousness of God, the question of the deepest interest and consequence to us, is *our personal relation to that righteousness*. Is righteousness in any degree inherent in human nature? If so, how may it be cultivated and developed? If not, is there any way of obtaining it? If so, by what means, and when?

To the mind untaught and unenlightened by the Word of God, this is a great, dark, baffling problem. In endeavoring to solve it, man has surely "sought out many inventions." But uncertainty and confusion regarding our relation to the righteousness of God are quite unnecessary, for the true situation is clearly stated in the Scriptures of Truth.

The Scriptures declare that "all have sinned, and come short of the

16

glory of God" (Rom. 3:23); that we are "carnal, sold under sin" (Rom. 7:14); that "there is none righteous, no, not one" (Rom. 3:10); that in our flesh there "dwelleth no good thing" (Rom 7:18); and finally, that we are "filled with all unrighteousness" (Rom. 1:29). This clearly answers the question as to whether righteousness is in any degree inherent in human nature. It is not. On the contrary, human nature is filled with unrighteousness.

But in this same Word we find the good, glad news that God has provided a way by which we may be cleansed from our unrighteousness, and be clothed and filled with His perfect righteousness. We find that this provision was made and revealed to Adam as soon as he fell from his high and holy estate. This merciful provision has been understood and laid hold of by fallen, unrighteous men and women from the very beginning of the fierce, unequal conflict with sin. This we learn from the following testimonies recorded in the Scriptures:

1. In one of His sermons, Christ refers to the second son of Adam, and speaks of him as "righteous Abel." Matt. 23:35. And Paul declares that Abel "obtained witness that he was righteous." Heb. 11:4

2. "The Lord said unto Noah, Come thou and all thy house into the ark; for thee have I seen righteous before Me in this generation." Gen. 7:1. Again: "Noah was a just man and perfect in his generations, and Noah walked with God." Gen. 6:9.

3. "Abraham believed God, and it was counted unto him for righteousness." Rom. 4:3.

4. "And delivered righteous Lot, sore distressed by the lascivious life of the wicked (for that righteous man dwelling among them, in seeing and hearing, vexed his righteous soul from day to day with their lawless deeds)." 2 Peter 2:7, 8, R.V.

5. Of Zacharias and Elisabeth, living just before the birth of Christ, it is said: "They were both righteous before God, walking in all the commandments and ordinances of the Lord blameless." Luke 1:6

6. The apostle Paul declares that the Gentiles to whom he had

preached the gospel had "attained to righteousness." Rom. 9:30; 6:17-22.

Thus it is seen that from the promise made to Adam, to the close of apostolic times, there were men and women all along the way who laid hold of the righteousness of God and had the evidence that their lives were pleasing to Him.

Upon What Conditions?

How was this accomplished? Upon what conditions was this wonderful transaction wrought? Was it because the times and conditions in which these men and women lived were favorable to righteousness? Or was it due to the special and superior qualities inherent in those who reached the high table-lands of godliness?

All the records of the times and of individuals give a negative answer. They were people with natures like our own, and their environment "vexed" their righteous souls from day to day. 2 Peter 2: 7, 8. They obtained the priceless blessing of righteousness in the one way, the only way, it has been possible for any human being to secure it since Adam sinned.

The way of being made righteous is given great prominence in the New Testament. The clearest and fullest exposition is found in the epistle of Paul to the Romans. At the very beginning of his argument the apostle declares: "I am not ashamed of the gospel of Christ: for it is the power of God unto salvation to every one that believeth. . . . For therein is the righteousness of God revealed from faith to faith: as it is written, The just shall live by faith." Rom. 1:16, 17.

It is the gospel that reveals to men the perfect righteousness of God. The gospel also reveals the way that righteousness may be obtained by sinful men, namely, by faith. This is presented at greater length in the following statement:

"By the deeds [the works] of the law there shall no flesh be justified [accounted righteous] in His sight: for by the law is the knowledge of sin. But now the righteousness of God without the law [works of the law] is manifested, being witnessed [approved, accepted] by the law and the prophets; even the righteousness of God which is by faith of Jesus Christ unto all and upon all them that believe." Rom. 3:20-22.

In the first part of this statement, the apostle shows the part which the law takes in the problem of justification. "By the law is the knowledge of sin." The *knowledge* of sin; not the *deliverance* from sin. The law points out sin. In so doing it declares the whole world to be guilty before God. Romans 3. But the law cannot deliver from sin. No effort of the sinner to obey the law can cancel his guilt or bring to him the righteousness of God.

That righteousness, Paul declares, is "by faith of Jesus Christ. . . . whom God hath set forth to be a propitiation [an atoning sacrifice] through faith in His blood, to declare His righteousness for the remission of sins that are past, through the forbearance of God." Rom. 3:22-25.

It is through faith in the blood of Christ that all the sins of the believer are canceled and the righteousness of God is put in their place to the believer's account. O, what a marvelous transaction! What a manifestation of divine love and grace! Here is a man born in sin. As Paul says, he is "filled with all unrighteousness." His inheritance of evil is the worst imaginable. His environment is at the lowest depths known to the wicked. In some way the love of God shining from the cross of Calvary reaches that man's heart. He yields, repents, confesses, and by faith claims Christ as his Saviour. The instant that is done, he is accepted as a child of God. His sins are all forgiven, his guilt is canceled, he is accounted righteous, and stands approved, justified, before the divine law. And this amazing, miraculous change may take place in one short hour. This is *righteousness by faith.*

Having made these clear, forceful statements as to the way of being made righteous, the apostle then illustrates the truth declared by a concrete case. He takes the experience of Abraham as an example.

"What shall we say then that Abraham our father, as pertaining to the flesh, hath found?" Rom. 4:1.

Anticipating his answer, we reply: Abraham had found righteousness. But how—by what method? Paul tells us:

"If Abraham were justified [accounted righteous] by works, he hath whereof to glory; but not before God." Rom. 4:2

Made righteous *by works* is a suggestion, a proposal,--*if* such a thing could be. Is that *the* way by which to obtain righteousness?

"What saith the scripture? Abraham believed God, and it [his belief] was counted unto him for righteousness." Rom. 4:3.

This statement settles forever the way by which Abraham obtained God's righteousness. It was *not by works*; it *was by faith*.

Abraham's Way the Only Way

Having settled the question as to how Abraham secured the righteousness of God, Paul proceeds to show that that is the only way anyone else can obtain righteousness.

"To him that worketh not, but believeth on Him that justifieth the ungodly, his faith is counted for righteousness.' Rom. 4:5.

What kindness! What great compassion! The Lord, who is "righteous in all His ways," offers His own perfect righteousness to any and every poor, weak, helpless, hopeless sinner who will believe what He says. Read it again: *"To him that worketh not, but believeth on Him. . . . his faith is counted for righteousness."*

So important, so fundamental is this way of righteousness that the apostle goes on through this entire chapter to restate and repeat and press home to all what he has made so clear in few words. Here are some of his statements:

"Even as David also describeth the blessedness of the man, unto whom God imputeth righteousness without works." Rom. 4:6.

"We say that faith was reckoned to Abraham for righteousness." Rom. 4:9.

"And being fully persuaded that, what he had promised, He was able also to perform. And therefore it was imputed to him for righteousness. Now it was not written for his sake alone, that it was imputed to him; but for us also, to whom it shall be imputed, if we believe on Him that raised up Jesus our Lord from the dead; who was delivered for our offenses [sins], and was raised again for our justification [righteousness]." Rom. 4:21-25.

This clear-cut, positive statement reveals to every lost soul for all time the only way from sin and guilt and condemnation to righteousness and deliverance from condemnation and death. With this agree all the other statements of the Scriptures regarding this great problem of being made righteous.

The three words, "righteousness of faith," express the most wonderful transaction in this material world which the human intellect can grasp. They express the greatest gift that God, in His infinite plenitude, could bestow upon mankind. The great fact expressed by this phrase of three words, has been studied, expounded, and rejoiced in by millions during past ages, and it is still the theme of the most sublime interest and importance to the human family.

Reviewing these statements, we find:

That the law of God demands righteousness from all who are under its jurisdiction. But through transgression all have made themselves incapable of rendering the righteousness which the law demands. What, then, is the sinner to do? His transgression of God's righteous law has made him unrighteous. This has brought him under the condemnation of that law. Being condemned, the penalty of his transgression must be paid. The penalty is death. He owes a debt that demands his life. He is under a condemnation that he can never remove. He is facing a penalty he can never escape. What can he do? Is here any way out of this dark, hopeless situation? Yes, there is.

The righteousness of God without the law is manifested, being witnessed [approved and accepted] by the law and the prophets; even the righteousness of God which is by faith of Jesus Christ unto all and upon all them that believe." Rom. 3:21, 22.

This reveals the way of meeting the demands of the law, and emphatically states that the only way of doing so is "by faith." To the natural, unilluminated mind, this solution of the dark problem is a mystery. The law requires obedience; it demands righteous deeds in the activities of life. How can such demands be met by faith instead of by works? The answer is given in plain words:

"Being justified freely by His grace through the redemption that is in Christ Jesus: whom God hath set forth to be a propitiation [an atoning sacrifice] through faith in His blood, to declare His righteousness for the remission of sins that are past, through the forbearance of God." Rom. 3:24, 25.

What a marvelous solution of the awful problem of sin! Only our infinite, all-wise, and compassionate Father could and would provide such a solution. Only inspired writings could reveal it. And this way of making a sinner righteous is found only in the untainted gospel of Christ.

"*By faith* he [the sinner, who has so grievously wronged and offended God] can bring to God the merits of Christ, and the Lord places the obedience of His Son to the sinner's account. Christ's righteousness is accepted in place of man's failure."– *Review and Herald, Nov. 4, 1890.*

Christ came to this world as our Redeemer. He became our substitute. He took our place in the conflict with Satan and sin. He was tempted in all points as we are, but never sinned. He loved righteousness and hated iniquity. His life of perfect obedience met the highest demands of the law. And O, the wonder and the marvel of it is that God accepts Christ's righteousness in the place of our failure, our unrighteousness!

In this divine transaction, "God receives, pardons, justifies, . . . and loves him [the sinner] as He loves His son."–*Ibid.* No wonder Paul proclaimed to the whole world that it was the love of Christ which constrained him in his arduous labors, and that he counted it a great privilege and joy to suffer the loss of all things, that he might gain Christ and stand clothed in His righteousness, which is imputed to the sinner through faith.

Thus is explained just *how* faith takes the place of works and is accounted righteousness. This wonderful truth should be perfectly clear to every believer; and it must become personal experience. It should enable us to cease from our own works, efforts, and struggles, and to enter into calm, trusting, living faith in the merits, the obedience, the righteousness of Christ. These we may present to God in the place of our failures. We should joyfully accept the pardon and justification granted, and should now experience the peace and joy which such a marvelous transaction is able to bring to our hearts.

"Therefore being justified [accounted righteous] by faith, we have peace with God through our Lord Jesus Christ." Rom. 5:1.

Many Have Missed the Way

How strange and how sad that this simple, beautiful way of righteousness seems so hard for the natural, carnal heart to find and accept! It was a great sorrow to Paul that Israel, his kinsman according to the flesh, missed the way so fatally. He said:

"Israel, which followed after the law of righteousness, hath not attained to the law of righteousness. Wherefore? Because they sought it not by faith, but as it were by the works of the law." Rom. 9:31, 32.

On the other hand, "the Gentiles, which followed not after righteousness, have attained to righteousness, even the righteousness which is of faith." Rom. 9:30.

And now the apostle reveals the real secret of Israel's failure:

"For they being ignorant of *God's righteousness, and going about to establish their own righteousness,* have not submitted themselves unto the righteousness of God. For Christ is the end of the law [the one to whom the law points] for righteousness to everyone that believeth." Rom. 10:3, 4.

Finally, the apostle closes his exposition of this sublime theme with these assuring words:

"But what saith it? The word is nigh thee, even in thy mouth, and in thy heart: that is, the word of faith, which we preach; that if thou shalt

23

confess with thy mouth the Lord Jesus, and shalt believe in thine heart that God hath raised Him from the dead, thou shalt be saved. For with the heart man believeth unto righteousness; and with the mouth confession is made unto salvation." Rom. 10:8-10.

"Righteousness by faith" is not a *theory*. People may hold a theory about it, and at the same time be "ignorant of God's righteousness and going about to establish their own righteousness." "Righteousness by faith" is a transaction, *an experience*. It is a submitting unto "the righteousness of God." It is a change of standing before God and His law. It is a regeneration, a new birth. Without this change there can be no hope for the sinner, for he will remain under the condemnation of God's changeless, holy law; its terrible penalty will still hang over his head.

How very essential it thus appears that we come to know, by clear, positive experience, that this great, vital transaction called "righteousness by faith" has been wrought in our hearts and lives by the power of God. Only then can we truly pray our Lord's prayer, addressing, "Our Father, who art in heaven, hallowed be Thy name."

> "This name is hallowed by the angels of heaven, by the inhabitants of unfallen worlds. When you pray, 'Hallowed be Thy name,' you ask that it may be hallowed in this world, hallowed in you. God has acknowledged you before men and angels as His child; pray that you may do no dishonor to the 'worthy name by which ye are called.' God sends you into the world as His representatives. In every act of life you are to make manifest the name of God. This petition calls upon you to possess His character. You cannot hallow His name, you cannot represent Him to the world, unless in life and character you represent the very life and character of God. This you can do only through the acceptance of the grace of righteousness of Christ." –*"Thoughts from the Mount of Blessing," p. 158.*

Part II

The Witness of the Spirit of Prophecy

"Urge them to give their attention to securing the richest gift that can be given to mortal Man.—the robe of Christ's righteousness."–*Testimonies,*" *Vol. IX, p. 114*

"All who assume the ornaments of the sanctuary, but are not clothed with Christ's righteousness, will appear in the shame of their own nakedness."–*Id. Vol. V, p. 81.*

Chapter Two

A Message of Supreme Importance

Nearly forty years ago (in 1888) there came to the Seventh-day Adventist Church a very definite awakening message. It was designated at the time as "the message of Righteousness by Faith." Both the message itself and the manner of its coming made a deep and lasting impression upon the minds of ministers and people, and the lapse of time has not erased that impression from memory. To this day, many of those who heard the message when it came are deeply interested in it and concerned regarding it. All these long years they have held a firm conviction, and cherished a fond hope, that some day this message would be given great prominence among us, and that it would do the cleansing, regenerating work in the church which they believed it was sent by the Lord to accomplish.

Among the influences which have led to this conviction is the divine witness borne to the proclamation of the message of Righteousness by Faith as it was set forth at the time of the General Conference held in the city of Minneapolis, Minn., in the year 1888. From the very first, the spirit of prophecy placed the seal of approval upon the message and its presentation at that time. In the plainest and most positive language we were told that the Lord was leading and impelling men to proclaim this definite message of Righteousness by Faith. Of that epochal Conference, and the men who gave the specific message, it is declared:

"The Lord in His great mercy sent a most precious message to His people. . . . This message was to bring more prominently before the

27

world the uplifted Saviour, the sacrifice for the sins of the whole world. It presented justification through faith in the Surety; it invited the people to receive the righteousness of Christ, which is made manifest in obedience to all the commandments of God. Many had lost sight of Jesus. They needed to have their eyes directed to His divine person, His merits, and His changeless love for the human family. All power is given into His hands, that he may dispense rich gifts unto men, imparting the priceless gift of His own righteousness to the helpless human agent. This is the message that God commanded to be given to the world. It is the third angel's message, which is to be proclaimed with a loud voice, and attended with the outpouring of His Spirit in a large measure."–*"Testimonies to Ministers," pp. 91, 92.*

Every sentence in this comprehensive statement is worthy of most careful study. Let us briefly analyze it:

1. A most Precious Message.—"The Lord in His great mercy sent a most precious message to his people."

2. The Object.—"This message was to bring more prominently before the world the uplifted Saviour, the sacrifice for the sins of the whole world."

3. The Scope.—

A, "It presented Justification through faith in the Surety."

B. "It invited the people to receive the righteousness of Christ, which is made manifest in obedience to all the commandments of God."

4. The Need.—

A. "Many had lost sight of Jesus."

B. "They needed to have their eyes directed to His divine person, His merits, and His changeless love for the human family."

5. The Resources.—

A. "All power is given into His hands,"

B. "That He May dispense rich gifts unto men,"

C. "Imparting the priceless gift of His own righteousness to the helpless human agent."

6. Extent.—"This is the message that God commanded to be given to the world."

7. What It Really Is.—"it is the third angel's message, which is to be proclaimed with a loud voice, and attended with the outpouring of His Spirit in a large measure."

It is difficult to conceive how there could be any misunderstanding or uncertainty regarding the heavenly endorsement of this message. It clearly stated that the Lord sent the message, and that He led the minds of the men who were so deeply engrossed by it and who proclaimed it with such earnestness.

It should be borne in mind at this time that the course taken by the messengers in subsequent years has nothing to do with the positive statement, oft repeated that they were led by the Lord to declare this fundamental truth of the gospel to His people at that particular time.

Not only was it in the purpose of God to set this message of Righteousness by Faith before his *church;* it was to be given to the *world.* And finally, it is declared to be the "third angel's message, which is to be proclaimed with a loud voice, and attended with the outpouring of His Spirit in a large measure." It is evident that the application of this message was not limited to the time of the Minneapolis Conference, but that its application extends to the close of time; and consequently it is of greater significance to the church at the present time than it could have been in 1888. The nearer we approach the great day of God, the more imperative will be the need of the soul-cleansing work which that message was sent to do. Surely we have every reason for a new, more earnest, whole-hearted study and proclamation of that message.

God's messages and providences are always great with meaning. They are always necessary for the accomplishment of the particular work with which they are connected. He orders them for the fulfilment of His purposes. They cannot be set aside. They cannot fail. Sooner or later they will be understood, accepted, and given their proper place. Therefore it must be expected that the message of

Righteousness by Faith, which came so definitely to the church in 1888, will be accorded a dominant place in the closing period of the great movement with which we are connected.

Chapter Three

Preparatory Messages

The Bible account of God's dealings with His people is full of most helpful instruction for the remnant church. It shows that through the centuries he has had but one unchangeable, eternal purpose. He has allowed nothing to defeat that purpose. In all the crises and developments that have arisen, He has been in control. He has foreseen the perils lurking along the way, and has sent warnings to His people to guard and protect them. When they have needed messages to awaken, inspire, and regenerate them, He has raised up messengers to give the messages. The great exodus movement from Egypt to Canaan, the history of Samuel and Israel, of David and the kingdom he was chosen to establish, and the tragic experiences of Jeremiah in the kingdom of Judah, and its overthrow and captivity, – all are illustrations of this.

In the records of these great crises we find that God's messages to the people were of a twofold character: *First*, they pointed out the deceptions into which His people were being led, and warned them of the serious results which would come unless they returned to Him; *second*, they revealed most clearly just what was needed to help them, and gave assurance that He would not only supply all their needs, but would also inspire and empower them to lay hold of the proffered help if they would but choose it with the whole heart. Nothing was lacking on the Lord's side to meet fully every deception and peril by which Satan sought to ruin the people and the cause.

The developments and experiences connected with the coming of the message of righteousness by Faith, in 1888, bear striking similarity to the experiences which came to the people of God in olden times. It is well to give most careful consideration to the messages of the spirit of prophecy just preceding the Minneapolis Conference of 1888.

The Messages of 1887

The testimonies of the spirit of prophecy which were received during the year 1887 gave warning of danger. They named again and again a specific evil, a deception into which the church was falling. That deception was pointed out as the fatal mistake of drifting into formalism; the substitution of forms, ceremonies, doctrines, machinery, and activities for the heart experience which comes alone through fellowship with Christ Jesus our Lord. Throughout the entire year this specific danger was kept before ministers and people by messages which appeared in the *Review and Herald*. In order that the seriousness of the situation at that time may be realized and the warnings better understood, we quote a few paragraphs, giving the date of publication:

1. "It is possible to be a formal, partial believer, and yet be found wanting, and lose eternal life. It is possible to practice some of the Bible injunctions, and be regarded as a Christian, and yet perish because you are lacking in essential qualifications that constitute Christian character."–*Review and Herald, Jan. 11, 1887*.

2. Two weeks later another message declares: "The observance of external forms will never meet the great want of the human soul. A mere profession of Christ is not enough to prepare one to stand the test of the judgment."–*Review and Herald, Jan. 25, 1887*.

3. Three weeks following this it was clearly stated: "There is too much formality in the church. Souls are perishing of light and knowledge. We should be so connected with the Source of light that we can be channels of light to the world. . . . Those who profess to be guided by the Word of God, may be familiar with the evidences of their faith, and yet be like the pretentious fig tree, which flaunted its foliage in the face of the world, but when

searched by the Master, was found destitute of fruit."–*Review and Herald, Feb. 15, 1887*

4. Two weeks thereafter came another of like import: "The Lord Jesus on the Mount of Olives, plainly stated that 'because iniquity shall abound, the love of many shall wax cold.' He speaks of a class who have fallen from a high state of spirituality. Let such utterances as these come home with solemn, searching power to our hearts. . . . A formal round of religious services is kept up; but where is the love of Jesus? Spirituality is dying. . . . Shall we meet the mind of the Spirit of God? Shall we dwell more upon practical godliness, and far less upon mechanical arrangements?"–*Written March 1, 1887; appears in 'Testimonies," Vol. V, pp. 538, 539.*

On and on throughout the entire year messages continued to come telling us that formality was coming into the church; that we were trusting too much in forms, ceremonies, theories, mechanical arrangements and a constant round of activities. Of course these messages were true, and they should have made a profound impression. But formalism is most deceptive and ruinous. It is the hidden, unsuspected rock upon which, through the centuries, the church has so often been well-nigh wrecked. Paul warns us that the "form of godliness" without the power of God will be one of the perils of the last days, and admonishes us to turn away from the deceptive, bewitching thing. Over and over again, and through various channels, God sends warnings to His church to escape the peril of formalism.

It was precisely this perilous deception against which the spirit of prophecy gave repeated warnings in 1887; and it was to save us from its full results that the message of righteousness by Faith was sent to us.

This movement is of God. It is destined to triumph gloriously. Its organization is heaven-indited; its departments are the wheels within the wheels, all skillfully linked together, but they are incomplete and partial without the Spirit within the wheels giving power and speedy results. These wheels are composed of men and women. God baptizes men and women rather than movements; and when men receive the power of the Spirit into their lives, then the beautiful machinery moves speedily forward on its appointed task. This must be realized individually before it can be realized collectively. How imperative, then, our need of God's provision!

But not alone came the warnings against the substitution of theories, forms, activities, and the machinery of organization. With these warnings came a direct, powerful, positive message telling exactly what should be done to save us from the situation into which we were drifting. The entire message cannot be reproduced here because of its length. It appears in full in the Appendix. (See pages: 112-118.) However, a few excerpts will convey some idea of its serious import, and of the hope it held out to the church if the instruction were heeded:

Greatest and Most Urgent Need

"A revival of true godliness among us is the greatest and most urgent of all our needs. To seek this should be our first work. There must be earnest effort to obtain the blessing of the Lord, not because God is not willing to bestow His blessing upon us, but because we are unprepared to receive it. . . .

"There are persons in the church who are not converted, and who will not unite in earnest, prevailing prayer. We must enter upon the work individually. We must pray more, and talk less. Iniquity abounds, and the people must be taught not to be satisfied with a form of godliness without the spirit and power. . . .

"We have far more to fear from within than from without. The hindrances to strength and success are far greater from the church itself than from the world. . . .

"There is nothing that Satan fears so much as that the people of God shall clear the way by removing every hindrance, so that the Lord can pour out His Spirit upon a languishing church and an impenitent congregation. If Satan had his way, there would never be another awakening, great or small, to the end of time. But we are not ignorant of his devices. It is possible to resist his power. When the way is prepared for the Spirit of God, the blessing will come. Satan can no more hinder a shower of blessing from descending upon God's people than he can close the windows of heaven that rain cannot come upon the earth. Wicked men and devils cannot hinder the work of God, or shut out His presence from the assemblies of His people, if they will, with subdued, contrite hearts, confess and put away their sins, and in faith claim His promises. Every temptation, every opposing influence, whether open or secret, may be successfully resisted, 'not by might nor by power, but by My Spirit, saith the Lord of hosts.'

"What is our condition in this fearful and solemn time? Alas, what pride is prevailing in the church, what hypocrisy, what deception, what love of dress, frivolity, and amusement, what desire for the supremacy! All these sins have clouded the mind, so that eternal things have not been discerned."–*Review and Herald*, March 22, 1887.

What a solemn message, and yet how full of tender, helpful counsel! What hope is held before the church if she will but sincerely heed it! How sad that this great message passed with annual files of the *Review*, to lie buried so long! Is it not time to bring again this message clearly and forcefully to the attention of the church, as Ezra brought forth the forgotten book of the law of Moses and read the instruction it contained to Israel?

The Remedy to Be Applied

As the year closed, a message came, pointing clearly and positively to the only remedy for the evils so earnestly and repeatedly set before us during the entire year. That remedy, we are told, is union with Christ Jesus the Lord.

"There is a wide difference between a pretended union and a real connection with Christ by faith. A profession of religion places men in the church, but this does not prove that they have a vital connection with the living Vine. . . . When this intimacy of connection and communion is formed, our sins are laid upon Christ, His righteousness is imputed to us. He was made sin for us, that we might be made the righteousness of God in Him.

"The power of evil is so identified with human nature that no man can overcome except by union with Christ. Through this union we receive moral and spiritual power. If we have the Spirit of Christ, we shall bring forth the fruit of righteousness. . . .

"A union with Christ by living faith is enduring; every other union must perish. Christ first chose us, paying an infinite price for our redemption; and the true believer chooses Christ as first and last, and best in everything. But this union costs us something. It is a relation of utter dependence, to be entered into by a proud being. All who form this union must feel their need of the atoning blood of Christ. They must have a change of heart. They must submit their own will to the will of God. There will be a struggle with outward and internal obstacles. There must be a painful work of detachment, as well as a work of attachment. Pride, selfishness, vanity, worldliness—sin in all its forms must be overcome, if we would enter into a union with Christ. The reason why many find the Christian life so deplorably hard, why they are so fickle, so variable, is they try to attach themselves to Christ without first detaching themselves from these cherished idols."—*Review and Herald, Dec. 13, 1887.*

This message takes us into the very heart of the gospel—union with Christ. No man can overcome sin except by this union. By union with Christ, our sins are laid upon Him and His righteousness is imputed to us. This is *reality*, not form nor ceremony. It is not church membership, nor assent of the intellect to theory and dogma. Union with Christ is a satisfying reality in all that pertains to the Christian life. In this lies our security. This was our great need in 1887, and to lead us into that experience the Lord sent the message of Righteousness by Faith.

The Messages of 1888

As we pass into year 1888, the positive, remedial messages which began in 1887 were continued, growing in clarity and force, as will be observed. The true way is clearly set forth,—the only way that gives genuine sincerity, reality, and victory. This true way is through fellowship with our risen Lord. Note the following ringing words:

The Only True Way

"Without the presence of Jesus in the heart, religious service is only dead, cold formalism. The longing desire for communion with God soon ceases when the Spirit of God is grieved from us; but when Christ is in us the hope of glory, we are constantly directed to think and act in reference to the glory of God."–*Review and Herald, April 17, 1888.*

"We should study the life of our Redeemer, for He is the only perfect example for men. We should contemplate the infinite sacrifice of Calvary and behold the exceeding sinfulness of sin and the righteousness of the law. You will come from a concentrated study of the theme of redemption strengthened and ennobled. Your comprehension of the character of God will be deepened; and with the whole plan of salvation clearly defined in your mind, you will be better able to fulfil your divine commission. From a sense of thorough conviction, you can then testify to men of the immutable character of the law manifested by the death of Christ on the cross, the malignant nature of sin, and the righteousness of God in justifying the believer in Jesus on condition of his future obedience to the statutes of God's government in heaven and earth." –*Review and Herald, April 24, 1888.*

Our Redeemer, His atoning sacrifice for us, the malignant nature of sin, the righteousness of Christ to be received by faith,–in the serious contemplation and full acceptance of these vital truths of the gospel are to be found pardon, justification, peace, joy, and victory.

A Startling Message

Following the pointing out of the only true way, there came a startling message that must have been designed of the Lord to lead His people to sense their peril and step quickly into the way of security:

"The solemn question should come home to every member of our churches, How are we standing before God, as the professed followers of Jesus Christ? Is our light shining forth to the world in clear, steady rays? Have we, as a people solemnly dedicated to God, preserved our union with the Source of all light? Are not the symptoms of decay and declension painfully visible in the midst of the Christian churches of today? Spiritual death has come upon the people that should be manifesting life and zeal, purity and consecration, by the most earnest devotion to the cause of truth. The facts concerning the real condition of the professed people of God, speak more loudly than their profession, and make it evident that some power has cut the cable that anchored them to the Eternal Rock, and that they are drifting away to sea, without chart or compass."–*Review and Herald, July 24, 1888.*

Some power, it is declared, had cut the cable that anchored the church to the Eternal Rock, and its members were drifting away to sea without chart or compass. What situation could be more alarming than this? What more convincing reason could be given to show the need of turning with all the heart to Him who alone is able to hold us fast?

Back to Safe Anchorage

Next came a message telling just what was necessary in order to repair the cable the enemy had cut, and thus bring us back to safe anchorage. Read it with care:

"It is not enough to be familiar with the arguments of the truth alone. You must meet the people through the life that is in Jesus. Your work will be made wholly successful if Jesus is abiding with you, for He has said, 'Without Me ye can do nothing.' Jesus stands knocking, knocking at the door of your hearts, and yet, for all this, some say continually, 'I cannot find Him.' Why not? He says, 'I stand here knocking.' Why do you not open the door, and say, 'Come in, dear Lord'? I am so glad for these simple directions as to the way to find Jesus. If it were not for them, I should not know how to find Him whose presence I desire so much. Open the door now, and empty the soul-temple of the buyers and sellers, and invite the Lord to come in. Say to Him, 'I will love Thee with all my soul. I will work the works of righteousness. I will obey the law of God.' Then you will feel the peaceful presence of Jesus."–*Review and Herald, Aug. 28, 1888.*

The Climax of the Preparatory Messages

Just a few weeks before the General Conference assembled at Minneapolis, the Lord sent the following message as an impressive climax to all the instruction that had been coming on this one great theme month after month for nearly two years:

"What is the work of the minister of the gospel? It is to rightly divide the word of truth; not to invent a new gospel, but to rightly divide the gospel already committed to them. They cannot rely upon old sermons to present to their congregations; for these set discourses may not be appropriate to meet the occasion or the wants of the people. There are subjects that are sadly neglected, that should be largely dwelt upon. The burden of our message should be the mission and life of Jesus Christ. Let there be a dwelling upon the humiliation, self-denial, meekness, and lowliness of Christ, that proud and selfish hearts may see the difference between themselves and the Pattern, and may be humbled. Show to your hearers Jesus in his condescension to save fallen man. Show them that he who was their surety had to take human nature, and carry it through the darkness and the fearfulness of the malediction of His Father, because of man's transgression of His law; for the Saviour was found in fashion as a man.

"Describe, if human language can, the humiliation of the Son of God, and think not that you have reached the climax, when you see Him exchanging the throne of light and glory which He had with the Father, for humanity. He came forth from heaven to earth; and while on earth, He bore the curse of God as surety for the fallen race. He was not obliged to do this. He chose to bear the wrath of God, which man had incurred through disobedience to the divine law. He chose to endure the cruel mockings, the deridings, the scourging, and the crucifixion.. 'And being found in fashion as a man, He humbled Himself, and became obedient unto death;' but the manner of His death was an astonishment to the universe, for it was 'even the death of the cross.' Christ was not insensible to ignominy and disgrace. He felt it all most bitterly. He felt it as much more deeply and acutely than we can feel suffering, as His nature was more exalted, and pure, and holy than that of the sinful race for whom He suffered. He was the Majesty of heaven; He was equal with the Father. He was the commander of the hosts of angels, yet He died for man the death that was, above all others, clothed with ignominy and reproach. O that the haughty hearts of men might realize this! O that they might enter into the meaning of redemption, and seek to learn the meekness and lowliness of Jesus."–*Review and Herald, Sept. 11, 1888.*

This instruction is directed especially to ministers–the teachers in Israel:

1. They were to rightly divide the word of truth.

2. They were not to invent a new gospel, but to rightly set forth the gospel already committed to them.

3. They were not to continue to preach their "old sermons" to the people, as these "set discourses" might not be appropriate to meet the wants of the people.

4. They were to dwell largely upon subjects that had been sadly neglected.

5. The burden of their message should be the mission and life of Jesus Christ.

The concluding paragraph furnishes a comprehensive outline of this sublime theme–the mission and life of Christ.

In Retrospect

At this distance it does seem as if all these direct, clear-cut, solemn messages should have made a more profound impression upon the minds of all the ministers. It would seem that they would have been fully prepared to listen to and drink in the timely, inspiring message of revival, reformation, and recovery that was presented with such clearness and in such sincere earnestness by the messengers whom the Lord raised up to deliver the message. The appropriation of the perfect righteousness of Christ by deceived, sinful hearts, was the remedy the Lord sent. It was just what was needed. Who can tell what would have come to the church and the cause of God if that message of Righteousness by Faith had been fully and whole-heartedly received by all at that time? And who can estimate the loss that has been sustained by the failure of many to receive that message? Eternity alone will reveal the whole truth regarding this matter.

Chapter Four

The Message Set Forth at the Minneapolis Conference

The message of Righteousness by Faith came clearly and fully into the open at the General Conference held at Minneapolis, Minn., in November, 1888. It was made the one great subject of study in the devotional part of the Conference. It would seem that the presentation of the subject had been anticipated, and that there was an understanding that it would receive a thorough discussion in the Conference. At any rate, that was what took place.

The message was not received alike by all who attended the Conference; in fact, there was serious differences of opinions concerning it among the leaders. This division of opinion may be classified as follows:

Class 1. – Those who saw great light in it and gladly accepted it; who believed it to be a most essential phase of the gospel, and felt that it should be given great emphasis in all efforts to save the lost. To this class the message appeared to be the real secret of a victorious life in the conflict with sin, and that the great truth of being made righteous by faith in the Son of God was the most pressing need of the remnant church in preparing for translation at the second advent.

Class 2. – There were some, however, who felt uncertain about the "new teaching," as they termed it. They seemed unable to grasp it. They could not reach a conclusion. As a result, their minds were thrown into a state of perplexity and confusion. They neither accepted nor rejected the message at the time.

Class 3. –But there were others who were decidedly opposed to the presentation of the message. They claimed that the truth of righteousness by faith had been recognized by our people from the very first, and this was true theoretically. For this reason they saw no occasion for placing such great stress and emphasis upon the subject as was being done by its advocates. Furthermore, they feared that the emphasis placed upon this theme of righteousness by faith would cast a shadow upon the doctrines that had been given such prominence from the beginning of our denominational history; and since they looked upon the preaching of those distinctive doctrines as the secret of the power and growth of our movement, they were fearful that if these doctrines were overshadowed by any teaching or message whatsoever, our cause would lose its distinctive character and force. Because of these fears, they felt it duty bound to safeguard both cause and people by decided opposition.

This difference of views among the leaders led to serious results. It created controversy, and a degree of estrangement which was most unfortunate. But through the intervening years there has been steadily developing the desire and hope –yes, the belief –that someday the message of Righteousness by Faith would shine forth in all its inherent worth, glory, and power, and receive full recognition. And during this same time, misapprehension and opposition have been disappearing. With many, there is now a pressing conviction that this message of Righteousness by Faith should be studied, taught, and stressed to the fullest extent that its importance demands.

No complete report of the presentation and discussion of the message of Righteousness by Faith at the Minneapolis Conference was published. Oral reports were given by those in attendance. But through subsequent writings of the spirit of prophecy, information is furnished regarding the developments in connection with the giving of the message and its reception and also its rejection, and it is quite necessary to become familiar with this inspired information in order to understand better our present situation. It would be far more agreeable to eliminate some of the statements given by the spirit of prophecy regarding the attitude of some of the leaders toward the message and the messengers. But this cannot be done without giving only a partial presentation of the situation which developed at the Conference, thus leaving the question in more or less of mystery.

The Source From Which the Message Came

It became necessary for positive assurance to be given that the message of Righteousness and Justification by Faith that came at that time was by the direct leading of God, because of the confusion that had resulted by the opposition raised against it. The statements which follow should remove all question of doubt regarding the source of the message set forth at the Minneapolis Conference:

"The present message –Justification by Faith –is a message from God; it bears the divine credentials, for its fruit is unto holiness." – *Review and Herald, Sept. 3, 1889.*

"Messages bearing the divine credentials have been sent to God's people; the glory, the majesty, the righteousness of Christ, full of goodness and truth, have been presented; the fullness of the Godhead in Jesus Christ has been set forth among us with beauty and loveliness, to charm all whose hearts are not closed with prejudice. We know that God has wrought among us. We have seen souls turned from sin to righteousness; we have seen faith revived in the hearts of the contrite ones." –*Review and Herald, May 27, 1890.*

Its Varied Reception

As previously stated, some who attended the Minneapolis Conference received the message of Righteousness by Faith with great satisfaction. It was to them a message of life. It gave them a new appreciation of Christ, a new vision of His great sacrifice on the cross. It brought to their hearts peace and joy and hope. It was the supreme element needed to prepare a people to meet God.

These individuals returned to their churches with a new unction to preach the gospel of salvation from sin, and to help their brethren to accept by faith the righteousness of Christ as revealed in the gospel. Sister White herself took a very active earnest part in this work, and reported through the *Review* some of her experiences. For example:

"We thank the Lord with all the heart that we have precious light to present before the people, and we rejoice that we have a message for this time which is present truth. The tidings that Christ is our righteousness has brought relief to many, many souls, and God says to His people, 'Go forward.' The message to the Laodicean church is applicable to our condition. How plainly is pictured the position of those who think they have all the truth, who take pride in their knowledge of the Word of God, while its sanctifying power has not been felt in their lives. The fervor of the love of God is wanting in their hearts, but it is this very fervor of love that makes God's people the light of the world.
. . .

"In every meeting since the General Conference, souls have eagerly accepted the precious message of the righteousness of Christ. We thank God that there are souls who realize that they are in need of something which they do not possess, —gold of faith and love, white raiment of Christ's righteousness, eye-salve of spiritual discernment. If you possess these precious gifts, the temple of the human soul will not be like a desecrated shrine. Brethren and sisters, I call upon you in the name of Jesus Christ of Nazareth, to work where God works. Now is the day of gracious opportunity and privilege." –*Review and Herald, July 23, 1889.*

Eight months later this word from her pen appeared:

"I have traveled from place to place, attending meetings where the message of the righteousness of Christ was preached. I considered it a privilege to stand by the side of my brethren, and give my testimony with the message for the time; and I saw that the power of God attended the message wherever it was spoken." –*Review and Herald, March 18, 1890.*

Of a meeting in South Lancaster she stated:

I have never seen a revival work go forward with such thoroughness, and yet remain so free from all undue excitement. There was no urging or inviting. The people were not called forward, but there was a solemn realization that Christ came not to call the righteous, but sinners, to repentance. The honest in heart were ready to confess their sins, and to bring forth fruit to God by repentance and restoration, as far as it lay in their power. We seemed to breathe in the very atmosphere of heaven. Angels were indeed hovering around. Friday evening, the social service began at five, and it was not closed until nine. . . . There were many who testified that as the searching truths had been presented, they had been convicted in the light of the law as transgressors. They had been trusting in their own righteousness. Now they saw it as filthy rags, in comparison with the righteousness of Christ, which is alone acceptable to God. While they had not been open transgressors, they saw themselves depraved and degraded in heart. They had substituted other gods in the place of their heavenly Father. They had struggled to refrain from sin, but had trusted in their own strength. We should go to Jesus just as we are, confessing our sins, and cast our helpless souls upon our compassionate Redeemer. This subdues the pride of the heart, and is a crucifixion of self." –*Review and Herald, March 5, 1889.*

What a mighty revival of true godliness, what a restoration of spiritual life, what a cleansing from sin, what a baptism of the Spirit, and what a manifestation of divine power for the finishing of the work in our own lives and in the world, might have come to the people of God if all our ministers had gone forth from that Conference as did this loyal, obedient servant of the Lord!

The Opposition

How sad, how deeply regrettable, it is that this message of righteousness in Christ should, at the time of its coming, have met with opposition on the part of earnest, well-meaning men in the cause of God! The message has never been received, nor proclaimed, nor given free course as it should have been in order to convey to the church the measureless blessings that were wrapped within it. The seriousness of exerting such an influence is indicated through the reproofs that were given. These words of reproof and admonition should receive most thoughtful consideration at this time:

"God has raised up men to meet the necessity of this time who will 'cry aloud and spare not,' who will lift up their 'voice like a trumpet, and show My people their transgression, and the house of Jacob their sins.' Their work is not only to proclaim the law, but to preach the truth for this time, --the Lord our righteousness. . . .

"But there are those who see no necessity for a special work at this time. While God is working to arouse the people, they seek to turn aside the message of warning, reproof, and entreaty. Their influence tends to quiet the fears of the people, and to prevent them from awaking to the solemnity of this time. Those who are doing this, are giving the trumpet an uncertain sound. They ought to be awake to the situation, but they have become ensnared by the enemy." *–Review and Herald, Aug. 13, 1889.*

Mark the serious indictment which follows:

"You will meet with those who will say, 'You are too much excited over the matter. You are too much in earnest. You should not be reaching for the righteousness of Christ, making so much of that. You should preach the law.' As a people we have preached the law until we are as dry as the hills of Gilboa, that had neither dew nor rain. We must preach Christ in the law, and there will be sap and nourishment in the preaching that will be as food to the famishing flock of God. We must not trust in our own merits at all, but in the merits of Jesus of Nazareth." *–Review and Herald, March 11, 1890.*

Note also the serious implication in the following statements:

"Some of our brethren are not receiving the message of God upon this subject. They appear to be anxious that none of our ministers shall depart from their former manner of teaching the good old doctrines. We inquire, Is it not time that fresh light should come to the people of God, to awaken them to greater earnestness and zeal? The exceeding great and precious promises given us in the Holy Scriptures have been lost sight of to a great extent, just as the enemy of all righteousness designed that they should be. He has cast his own dark shadow between us and our God, that we may not see the true character of God." *– Review and Herald, April 1, 1890.*

"God has sent to His people testimonies of truth and righteousness, and they are called to lift up Jesus, and to exalt His righteousness. Those whom God has sent with a message are only men, but what is the character of the message which they bear? Will you dare to turn from, or make light of, the warnings, because God did not consult you as to what would be preferred? God calls men who will speak, who will cry aloud and spare not. God has raised up His messengers to do His work for this time. Some have turned from the message of the righteousness of Christ to criticize the men." –*Review and Herald, May 27, 1890.*

"The Lord has sent a message to arouse His people to repent, and do their first works; but how has His message been received? While some have heeded it, others have cast contempt and reproach on the message and the messenger. Spirituality deadened, humility and childlike simplicity gone, a mechanical, formal profession of faith has taken the place of love and devotion. Is this mournful condition of things to continue? Is the lamp of God's love to go out in darkness?" –*Review and Herald, Extra, Dec. 23, 1890.*

Lest we miss the force of these heart-searching messages, let us recount the salient points:

1. God raised up men to meet the necessity of the time.

2. Some sought to turn aside the message, and to prevent an awakening among the people.

3. Such persons were ensnared by the enemy, and gave the trumpet an uncertain sound.

4. These men declared that the law should be preached, –not the righteousness of Christ.

5. The exhortation is to *preach Christ in the law.*

6. Some were fearful of a departure from the former manner of preaching the good old doctrines.

7. God raised up men to herald the message of Righteousness by Faith.

8. The challenge: 'Will you dare to turn from, or make light of, the warnings?"

9. The twofold result of rejecting the message:

A. Deadening of spirituality.

B. Influx of a mechanical, formal profession of faith.

10. The climactic question: "Is this mournful condition of things to continue?"

Verily it is a sobering resume!

The Results of Division of Opinion

The division and conflict which arose among the leaders because of the opposition to the message of righteousness in Christ, produced a very unfavorable reaction. The rank and file of the people were confused and did not know what to do. Concerning this reaction, we read:

If our brethren were all laborers together with God, they would not doubt but that the message He has sent us during these last two years is from heaven. Our young men look to our older brethren, and as they see that they do not accept the message, but treat it as though it were of no consequence, it influences those who are ignorant of the Scriptures to reject the light. These men who refuse to receive truth, interpose themselves between the people and the light. But there is no excuse for any one's refusing the light, for it has been plainly revealed. There is no need of any one's being in ignorance. . . . . Instead of pressing your weight against the chariot of truth that is being pulled up an inclined road, you should work with all the energy you can summon to push it on." –*Review and Herald, March 18, 1890.*

"For nearly two years, we have been urging the people to come up and accept the light and the truth concerning the righteousness of Christ, and they do not know whether to come and take hold of this precious truth or not. They are bound about with their own ideas. They do not let the Saviour in." –*Review and Herald, March 11, 1890.*

"Some have turned from the message of the righteousness of Christ to criticize the men. . . . The third angel's message will not be comprehended, the light which will lighten the earth with its glory will be called a false light, by those who refuse to walk in its advancing glory. The work that might have been done, will be left undone by the rejecters of truth, because of their unbelief. We entreat of you who oppose the light of truth, to stand out of the way of God's people. Let Heaven-sent light shine forth upon them in clear and steady rays." —*Review and Herald, May 27, 1890.*

"There is sadness in heaven over the spiritual blindness of many of our brethren. . . The Lord has raised up messengers and endued them with His spirit, and has said, 'Cry aloud, spare not, lift up thy voice like a trumpet, and show My people their transgression, and the house of Jacob their sins.' Let no one run the risk of interposing himself between the people and the message of heaven. The message of God will come to the people; and if there were no voice among men to give it, the very stones would cry out. I call upon every minister to seek the Lord, to put away pride, to put away strife after supremacy, and humble the heart before God. It is the coldness of heart, the unbelief of those who ought to have faith, that keeps the church in feebleness." —*Review and Herald, July 26, 1892.*

The solemn import of these heaven-indited words should not be missed. Mark well these crystal-clear statements:

1. The message of 1888-90 was from heaven.

2. Its rejection by some of the more experienced brethren led the younger men into uncertainty and confusion.

3. Those who rejected the message, interposed themselves between the people and the light.

4. There is no excuse; the light has been plainly revealed.

5. The reason men are slow to take hold of this precious truth is because they are bound about with their own ideas.

6. The course of some has been to turn from the message to criticize the messengers.

7. Those who refuse to walk in this advancing light, will be unable to comprehend the third angel's message.

8. Those who refuse to walk in this heavenly light, that is to lighten the earth with its glory, will call it a "false light."

9. As a result of their unbelief, important work will be left undone.

10. Solemn entreaty to those who oppose the light to *"stand out of the way"* of the people.

11. Such spiritual blindness causes "sadness in heaven."

12. The positive assurance that God "raised up messengers and endued them with His Spirit."

13. If there had been no human voice lifted to give the message, the very stones would have cried out.

14. The call to every minister to humble the heart before God in order that spiritual strength may come to the church.

Surely comment on such solemn warnings and entreaties would be superfluous.

Fundamental Principles Involved

Back of the opposition is revealed the shrewd plotting of that master-mind of evil, the enemy of all righteousness. The very fact of his determination to neutralize the message and its inevitable effects, is evidence of its great value and importance; and how terrible must be the results of any victory of his in defeating it! Concerning Satan's shrewd planning, we are given plain warning:

"The enemy of man and God is not willing that this truth [justification by faith] should be clearly presented; for he knows that if the people receive it fully, his power will be broken. If he can control minds so that doubt and unbelief and darkness shall compose the experience of those who claim to be the children of God, he can overcome them with temptation." –*Review and Herald, Sept. 3, 1889.*

"Our present position is interesting and perilous. The danger of refusing light from heaven should make us watchful unto prayer, lest we should any of us have an evil heart of unbelief. When the Lamb of God was crucified on Calvary, the death knell of Satan was sounded; and if the enemy of truth and righteousness can obliterate from the mind the thought that it is necessary to depend upon the righteousness of Christ for salvation, he will do it. If Satan can succeed in leading man to place value upon his own works as works of merit and righteousness, he knows that he can overcome him by his temptations, and make him his victim and prey. Lift up Jesus before the people. Strike the door-posts with the blood of Calvary's Lamb, and you are safe." –*Review and Herald, Sept. 3, 1889.*

Once more let us summarize these statements, because of their far-reaching importance:

1. It is Satan who is unwilling that the truth of righteousness by faith shall be presented.

2. The reason is that, if this truth is fully received by the people, his power will be broken.

3. If Satan can throw about the people doubt and unbelief, he can overcome them through temptation.

4. It is Satan's endeavor to obliterate from the mind that it is necessary to depend upon the righteousness of Christ for salvation.

5. If Satan can lead men to depend upon their own works for righteousness, he knows they will be his victims.

6. Therefore the call is sounded: Lift up the crucified Saviour, and place your trust in His blood.

What a challenge to prayer is here presented! How we should seek God in humility for the anointing of the heavenly eyesalve! Only by the full acceptance and appropriation of these glorious provisions can a people be prepared to stand without spot or wrinkle before a holy God at His coming. Only thus may His commandments be truly kept, and only by this divine power can the church finish its great commission.

Chapter Five

The Message of 1888 Marks a New Era in the Proclamation of the Third Angel's Message

Careful study of the instruction given by the spirit of prophecy leads to the deep conviction that the coming of the message of Righteousness by Faith at the Minneapolis Conference, was a signal providence of God, –a providence designed to initiate the beginning of a new era in the finishing of His work. The following statement, written just four years after the Minneapolis Conference in 1888, affords basis for this conclusion:

"The time of test is just upon us, for the loud cry of the third angel has already begun in the revelation of the righteousness of Christ, the sin-pardoning Redeemer. This is the beginning of the light of the angel whose glory shall fill the whole earth." –*Review and Herald*, Nov. 22, 1892.

Almost alarming in character are the statements in the foregoing paragraph. They have a very important bearing on the work Seventh-day Adventists are carrying forward, and therefore are of the greatest interest to all who are connected with the work of proclaiming the third angel's message. Let us reread the paragraph from an analytical stand-point:

1. The time of test is just upon us.

2. The *loud cry* of the third angel *has already begun.*

3. It began in the revelation of the righteousness of Christ (the message of 1888).

4. This marks the beginning of the light of the angel whose glory shall fill the whole earth.

The events mentioned in this paragraph are the same as those brought to view in Revelation 18: 1, 2:

"After these things I saw another angel come down from heaven, having great power; and the earth was lightened with his glory. And he cried mightily with a strong voice, saying, Babylon the great is fallen, is fallen, and is become the habitation of devils, and the hold of every foul spirit, and a cage of every unclean and hateful bird."

The explanation of this scripture, as given by the spirit of prophecy, should be carefully noted:

"I saw angels hurrying to and fro in heaven, descending to the earth, and again ascending to heaven, preparing for the fulfilment of some important event. Then I saw another mighty angel commissioned to descend to the earth, to unite his voice with the third angel, and give power and force to his message. Great power and glory were imparted to the angel, and as he descended, the earth was lightened with his glory. The light which attended this angel penetrated everywhere, as he cried mightily, with a strong voice. . . the work of this angel comes in at the right time to join in the last great work of the third angel's message, as it swells to a loud cry. And the people of God are thus prepared to stand in the hour of temptation, which they are soon to meet. I saw a great light resting upon them, and they united to fearlessly proclaim the third angel's message." –"*Early Writings,*" *p. 277.*

The panorama of events presented in the foregoing paragraph is so extensive and so full of meaning that it may be helpful to note each event separately:

1. A mighty angel comes down from heaven to earth.

2. The work of this angel is:

A. To unite his voice with the third angel

B. To give power and force to the third angel's message.

54

3. Great power and glory were imparted to this angel:

   A. The earth was lightened with his glory.

   B. The light penetrated everywhere.

4. The work of this mighty angel comes in at just the right time to join in the last great work of the third angel's message.

5. As a result of the coming of this mighty angel, the message swells into a loud cry.

6. The power attending this mighty angel prepares the people of God to stand in the hour of trial.

7. This preparation is recognized by heaven in the bestowal of "a great light" to rest upon God's people.

8. The culmination of all these events is a united people, fearlessly proclaiming the third angel's message.

Inseparably connected with this program of great events is the visitation of the "latter rain" upon the remnant church. Note the following paragraph:

"While the work of salvation is closing, trouble will be coming on the earth, and the nations will be angry, yet held in check so as not to prevent the work of the third angel. At that time the 'latter rain,' or refreshing from the presence of the Lord, will come, to give power to the loud voice of the third angel, and prepare the saints to stand in the period when the seven last plagues shall be poured out." –*"Early Writings,"* pp. 85, 86.

This places the latter rain visitation with the loud cry, the revelation of the righteousness of Christ, and the flooding of the earth with the light of the third angel's message.

This is a program of truly thrilling events. It was outlined by the spirit of prophecy at the very beginning of our movement. And then, to awaken and arouse us to its serious import, a most solemn and impressive message regarding the same events was given us following the memorable Conference of 1888. The following vital statements taken from that message will give emphasis to the subject under consideration:

1. An Eventful Period of Time.

"*The days in which we live are eventful and full of peril.* The signs of the coming of the end are thickening around us, and events are to come to pass that will be of a more terrible character than any the world has yet witnessed."

2. The "Loud Cry" Begins.

"*The time of test is just upon us, for the loud cry of the third angel has already begun in the revelation of the righteousness of Christ,* the sin-pardoning Redeemer. This is the beginning of the light of the angel whose glory shall fill the whole earth."

3. The essential Preparation to Stand in the Time of Trouble.

"If you would stand through the time of trouble, you must know *Christ and appropriate the gift of His righteousness,* which He imputes to the repentant sinner."

4. The Message to Be Preached.

"A work is to be accomplished in the earth similar to that which took place at the outpouring of the Holy Spirit in the days of the early disciples, when they *preached Jesus and Him crucified.* Many will be converted in a day; for the message will go with power."

"*The theme that attracts the heart of the sinner is Christ, and Him crucified.* On the cross of Calvary, Jesus stands revealed to the world in unparalleled love. *Present Him thus to the hungering multitudes,* and the light of His love will win men from darkness to light, from transgression to obedience and true holiness. Beholding Jesus upon the cross of Calvary arouses the conscience to the heinous character of sin as nothing else can do."

"Christ has not been presented in connection with the law as a faithful and merciful High Priest, who was in all points tempted like as we are, yet without sin. He has not been lifted up before the sinner as the divine sacrifice. His work as sacrifice, substitute, and surety, has been only coldly and casually dwelt upon; but this is what the sinner needs to know. *It is Christ in His fullness as a sin-pardoning Saviour,* that the sinner must see; for the unparalleled love of Christ, through the agency of the Holy Spirit, will bring conviction and conversion to the hardened heart."

5. The Power That Gives Efficiency to the Preaching.

"The work of the *Holy Spirit* is immeasurably great. It is from *this source that power and efficiency come to the worker* for God; and the Holy Spirit is the Comforter, as the personal presence of Christ to the soul."

"When the earth is lightened with the glory of God, we shall see a work similar to that which was wrought when the disciples, *filled with the Holy Spirit*, proclaimed the power of a risen Saviour."

"*The Revelation of Christ by the Holy Spirit* brought to them [the disciples] a realizing sense of His power and majesty, and they stretched forth their hands unto Him by faith, saying, 'I believe.' Thus it was in the time of the early rain; but the latter rain will be more abundant. The Saviour of men will be glorified, and the earth will be lightened with the bright shining of the beams of His righteousness." –*The foregoing five quotations are from the Review and Herald*, Nov. 22 and 29, 1892; article entitled, "*The Perils and Privileges of the last Days.*" (See appendix, pp. 124-130.)

It will be seen that all these events are associated together to be in operation at the same time. Placed in their natural order, they stand as follows:

1. The revelation and appropriation by faith of the righteousness of Christ.

2. The bestowal of the latter rain.

3. The impartation of great power to the receivers.

4. The swelling of the third angel's message into the "loud cry."

5. The enlightening of the earth with the "bright shining of the beams of righteousness."

It is evident that the beginning, or opening of all these events, is at the same time. The appearance of one is a signal for all to appear.

And now mark the positive declaration:

"The loud cry of the third angel has already begun in the revelation of the righteousness of Christ, the sin-pardoning Redeemer. This is the beginning of the light of the angel whose glory shall fill the whole earth." –*Review and Herald*, Nov. 22, 1892.

This was declared in 1892. What marked the fresh, or new, revelation of the righteousness of Christ and the beginning of the loud cry? As the statement itself points out, it was "the revelation of the righteousness of Christ" as set forth at the Minneapolis Conference.

Now these important manifestations are ordained of God for the finishing of His work in the earth. When they began, they marked the starting point for that closing work. That place, that hour, was reached in 1888.

This is a tremendous conclusion, but what other conclusion can be reached with all the statements before us? Why should this conclusion be thought incredible? We believe the statements to be true. We have looked for their fulfilment. Our waiting for the fulfilment has been anxious and long. The fulfilment will be witnessed by someone. Why may we not see it and be in it?

Should we not seek most seriously and earnestly to know what may be hindering the fulfilment in all hastening His work to its close?

Chapter Six

The Third Angel's Message in Verity

A serious question arose in the minds of some who heard the message of Righteousness by Faith presented at the Minneapolis Conference, as to the relation that message bore to the third angel's message. In their perplexity, a number wrote to Mrs. E. G. White for an expression of her views on this question.

Regarding this inquiry and her reply, we have her published statement, as follows:

"Several have written to me, inquiring if the message of justification by faith is the third angle's message, and I have answered, 'It is the third angel's message in verity.'" –*Review and Herald, April 1, 1890.*

There is more in this statement than a brief, clear, positive answer to a question. It has a deep, vital meaning. It sounds a serious warning, and makes an intelligent, earnest appeal to every believer in the third angel's message. Let us give the statement careful study.

Justification by faith, it is affirmed, is "the third angel's message in verity." The words "in verity" mean, *in fact, in reality, in very truth.* That means that the message of Justification by Faith and the third angel's message are the same in purpose, in scope, and in results.

Justification by faith is God's way of saving sinners; His way of convicting sinners of their guilt, their condemnation, and their utterly undone and lost condition. It is also God's way of canceling their guilt, delivering them from the condemnation of His divine law, and giving them a new and right standing before Him and His holy law. Justification by faith is God's way of changing weak, sinful, defeated men and women into strong, righteous, victorious Christians.

Now if it be true that justification by faith is "the third angel's message in verity," –in fact, in reality, --it must be that the genuine understanding and appropriation of the third angel's message is designed to do for and in those who receive it, the full work of justification by faith. That this is its purpose, is evident from the following considerations:

1. The great threefold message of Revelation 14, which we designate by the term "the third angel's message," is declared to be "the everlasting gospel." Rev. 14:6.

2. The message makes the solemn announcement that the "hour of His judgment is come."

3. It admonishes all who are to meet God at His great tribunal, to be judged by His righteous law, to "fear God, and give glory to Him," and to "worship Him that made heaven, and earth." Verse 7.

4. The result, or fruitage, of this message of warning and admonition is the development of a people of whom it is declared: "Here is the patience of the saints: here are they that keep the commandments of God, and the faith of Jesus." Verse 12.

In all this we have the facts of justification by faith. The message is the gospel of salvation from sin, condemnation, and death. The judgment brings men and women face to face with the law of righteousness, by which they are to be tried. Because of their guilt and condemnation, they are warned to fear and worship God. This involves conviction of guilt, repentance, confession, and renunciation. This is the ground of forgiveness, cleansing, and justification. Those who enter into this experience have had wrought into their characters the sweet, beautiful grace of patience, in an age of all-pervading irritability and fiery temper, which is destroying the peace, happiness, and safety of the human race. What is that but justification by faith? The word declares that, "Being justified by faith, we have peace with God through our Lord Jesus Christ." Rom. 5:1.

But more still, these believers "keep the commandments of God." They have experienced the marvelous change from hating and transgressing the law of God, to loving and keeping its righteous precepts. Their standing before the law has been changed. Their guilt has been canceled; their condemnation has been removed and the death sentence has been annulled. Having accepted Christ as Saviour, they have received His righteousness and his life.

This wondrous transformation can be wrought only by the grace and power of God, and it is wrought for those only who lay hold of Christ as their substitute, their surety, their Redeemer. Therefore, it is said that they "keep the faith of Jesus." This reveals the secret of their rich, deep experience. They laid hold of the faith of Jesus, –that faith by which He triumphed over the powers of darkness.

"When the sinner believes that Christ is his personal Saviour, then, according to His unfailing promises, God pardons his sin, and justifies him freely. The repentant soul realizes that his justification comes because Christ, as his substitute and surety, has died for him, is his atonement and righteousness." –*Review and Herald, Nov. 4, 1890.*

As already pointed out, we find in the experiences of those who triumph in the third angel's message all the facts of justification by faith. For this reason, it is quite true that justification by faith is "the third angel's message in verity."

And here it may be well to call attention to the fact that both justification by faith and the third angel's message are the gospel of Christ in verity. This is made apparent by a statement from the apostle Paul, who declares that the "gospel of Christ . . . is the power of God unto salvation to everyone that believeth. . . For therein is the righteousness of God revealed from faith to faith." Rom. 1:16, 17.

The facts here presented are these:

1. The gospel is a manifestation of God's power at work, delivering sinners from their sins and planting in them His own righteousness.

2. But this is done for those only who believe.

3. This is being made just, or righteous, by faith.

4. And this is the purpose of both the message of justification by faith and the third angel's message.

What, then is the important lesson to be gained from the statement we have had under examination? What is the warning it sounds? Plainly the following:

That all who accept the third angel's message should enter into the experience of justification by faith. They should have Christ revealed to and in them. They should know by personal experience the work of re-generation. They should have the fullest assurance that they have been born anew, from above, and that they have passed from death unto life. They should know that their guilt has been canceled, that they have been delivered from the condemnation of the law, and are thus ready to appear before the judgment seat of Christ. They should know by victori-ous experience that they have laid hold of, and are being kept by, "the faith of Jesus," and that by this faith they are empowered to keep the commandments of God.

To fail to enter into this experience, will be to miss the real, vital, redeeming virtue of the third angel's message. Unless this experience is gained, the believer will have only the theory, the doctrines, the forms and activities, of the message. That will prove a fatal and awful mistake. The theory, the doctrines, even the most earnest activities of the mes-sage, cannot save from sin, nor prepare the heart to meet God in judg-ment.

It is regarding the danger of making this fatal mistake that we are warned. Formalism,—having "the form of knowledge and of the truth in the law," without having a living experience in Christ, is the hidden rock that has wrecked untold thousands of professed followers of Christ. It is against this danger that we are seriously warned.

But there is more than warning in this statement. There is appeal also, —an earnest, winsome appeal to enter into fellowship with Christ Jesus our Lord. There is a call to the highest table-lands of Christian ex-perience. There is assurance that when justified by faith we shall have peace with God, and shall be able continually to rejoice in hope of the glory of God. There is promise that we shall not be put to shame by defeat in our conflict with sin, because the love of God has been shed abroad in our hearts by the Holy Spirit which has been given unto us. Rom. 5: 1-5.

O that we had all listened as we should to both warning and appeal as they came to us in that seemingly strange, yet impressive way at the Conference of 1888! What uncertainty would have been removed, what wanderings and defeats and losses would have been prevented! What light and blessing and triumph and progress would have come to us! But thanks be unto Him who loves us with an everlasting love, it is not too late even now to respond with the whole heart to both warning and appeal, and receive the great benefits provided.

Christ Our Righteousness

PART III

A Study of the Scope of the Subject

"A small key may open a very complex lock and a very large door, and that door itself may lead into a vast building with priceless stores of wealth and beauty." –Pierson.

Chapter Seven

A Fundamental, All-Embracing Truth

In Part II the subject of Righteousness by Faith has been dealt with largely in its historical aspect, —the time, the place, and the manner in which the Lord chose to bring His people face to face with this vital, fundamental truth of the gospel for the purpose of adding strength, power, and expansion to the proclamation of the third angel's message which had been so signally entrusted to them. We now come to an analysis of the subject in its broad aspects, as it is presented in the writings of the spirit of prophecy.

The Minneapolis Conference adjourned with the minds of the delegates in more or less uncertainty and confusion regarding the message of Righteousness by Faith that had been set forth. But the presentation of this vital truth, with all the agitation, discussion, and perplexity it occasioned, was not in vain by any means. It started new thought and study regarding the great theme of justification by faith, and led many into a better, richer appreciation of the Saviour as their substitute and surety. Among the greatest of all the blessings that have followed that meeting has been the abundant instruction which the Lord has sent to His people through the spirit of prophecy regarding our Lord and Saviour Jesus Christ and how to live His life by faith. This instruction is truly illuminating.

It is worthy of note that since the Minneapolis Conference there have come to us, through the spirit of prophecy, the following volumes of instruction:

"Steps to Christ," in 1892.

"Thoughts From the Mount of Blessing." In 1896.

"Christ's Object lessons," in 1900.

"The Ministry of Healing," in 1905.

"The Acts of the Apostles," in 1911.

It is well known to all who have read these books that the great dominant theme is Christ, —His victorious life in humanity, His atoning sacrifice on the cross, and how He now may be made unto us poor mortals, wisdom, righteousness, sanctification, and redemption.

Besides these intensely spiritual books, scores and scores of messages have been sent to us through the *Review and Herald,* which contain the clearest and most helpful instruction regarding the subject of righteousness by faith. All this is of priceless value to the church. It throws a flood of light upon the great problem of redemption in all its phases.

In studying further into the subject of righteousness by faith, as set forth in the spirit of prophecy, it is important that there should be a clear understanding of its scope. This is not a doctrine of limited intent or of minor consequence. It is not a subject with which one may or may not be familiar and fare as well. Righteousness by Faith, in its larger meaning, embraces every vital, fundamental truth of the gospel. It begins with man's moral standing when created, and deals with —

1. The law by which man is to live.

2. Transgression of that law.

3. Penalty for transgression.

4. Problem of redemption.

5. Love of Father and Son which made redemption possible.

6. Justice in accepting a substitute.

7. Nature of the atonement.

8. Incarnation.

9. Sinless life of Christ.

10. Vicarious death of the Son of God.

11. Burial, resurrection, and ascension.

12. The Father's assurance of a satisfactory substitution.

13. The coming of the Holy Spirit.

14. The ministry of Jesus in the heavenly sanctuary.

15. The part required of the sinner in order to be redeemed.

16. Nature of faith, repentance, confession, obedience.

17. Meaning and experience of regeneration, justification, and sanctification.

18. Need and place of the Holy Spirit and Word of God in making real to men what was made possible on the cross.

19. Victory over sin through the indwelling Christ.

20. Place of works in the life of the believer.

21. Place of prayer in receiving and holding the righteousness of Christ.

22. The culmination and deliverance in the return of the Redeemer.

This is the great sweep of truth embraced in the short phrase "righteousness by faith.' "A small key," says Pierson, "may open a very complex lock and a very large door, and that door itself may lead into a vast building with priceless stores of wealth and beauty." The brief phrase, "righteousness by faith," opens the door to all the priceless stores of wealth and glory of the gospel in Christ Jesus our Lord.

It is worthwhile to note at this point some of the expressions found in the writings of the spirit of prophecy which serve to introduce or provide appropriate framework for this beautiful truth.

It Bears the Divine Credentials

"The present message, justification by faith, is a message from God; it bears the divine credentials, for its fruit is unto holiness." *—Review and Herald, Sept. 3, 1889.*

A Precious Thought

"The thought that the righteousness of Christ is imputed to us, not because of any merit on our part, but as a free gift from God, seemed a precious thought." *—Review and Herald, Sept. 3, 1889.*

It Is Sweetest Melodies

"The sweetest melodies that come from human lips, —justification by faith, and the righteousness of Christ." *—Review and Herald, April 4, 1895.*

It Is a Pure White Pearl

"The righteousness of Christ, as a pure white pearl, has no defect, no stain, no guilt. This righteousness may be ours." *—Review and Herald, Aug. 8, 1899.*

In its truest sense, righteousness by faith is not a *theory*; it is an *experience*, a vital change which takes place in the believer in Christ. It gives the sinner a new standing before God. It is the essence of Christianity for we read:

"The sum and substance of the whole matter of Christian grace and experience is contained in believing on Christ, in knowing God and His Son whom He hath sent." "Religion means the abiding of Christ in the heart, and where he is, the soul goes on in spiritual activity, ever growing in grace, ever going on to perfection.' *—Review and Herald*, May 24, 1892.

To lose sight of this wonderful, fundamental, all-embracing truth is to miss that which is vital in the plan of redemption.

Chapter Eight

The Deadly Peril of Formalism

Interwoven all through the instruction given by the spirit of prophecy regarding the great importance of receiving, experiencing, and proclaiming the gracious truth of righteousness by faith, we find impressive warnings concerning the great peril for formalism.

Righteousness by faith is not formalism. The two are direct opposites. Righteousness by faith is an experience, a reality. It involves a complete transformation of the life. He who has entered into his new life has experienced deep contrition and has made sincere, heartfelt confession and repudiation of sin. With his divine Lord, he has come to love righteousness and hate iniquity. And being justified –accounted righteous by faith–he has peace with God. He is a new creature; old things have passed away, all things have become new.

Formalism is vastly different. It is of the head, and deals with externals. It stops with the theory of religion. It goes no deeper than the form and the pretense. Hence it is like salt without savor. It is a joyless, loveless religion, for it does not bring peace, assurance, and victory. Formalism springs from and thrives in the natural heart, where it has its root. It is one of those subtle, all-pervading evils which the Redeemer came to uproot and eliminate from the human heart.

Formalism has always been a real peril to the church. A Christian writer of modern times has referred to this subtle peril as follows:

"The gospel of externalism is dear to the human heart. It may take the form of culture and moralities; or of 'services' and sacraments and churchly order; or of orthodoxy and philanthropy. These and such

71

things make themselves our idols; and trust in them takes the place of faith in the living Christ. It is not enough that the eyes of our heart should have once seen the Lord, that we should in other days have experienced 'the renewing of the Holy Ghost.' It is possible to forget, possible to 'remove from Him that called us in the grace of Christ.' With little change in the form of our religious life, its inward reality of joy in God, of conscious sonship, of fellowship in the Spirit, may be utterly departed.

"The gospel of formalism will spring up and flourish on the most evangelical soil, and in the most strictly Pauline churches. Let it be banned and barred out never so completely; it knows how to find entrance, under the simplest modes of worship and the soundest doctrine. The serried defense of Articles and Confessions constructed against it will not prevent its entrance, and may even prove its cover and intrenchment. Nothing avails as the apostle says, but a constant 'new creation.' The life of God in human souls is sustained by the energy of His Spirit, perpetually renewed, ever proceeding from the Father and the Son. 'The life that I live in the flesh, I live by the faith of the Son of God, who loved me and gave Himself for me.' This is the true orthodoxy. The vitality of his personal faith in Christ kept Paul safe from error, faithful in will and intellect to the one gospel."—*G. G. Findlay, in his exposition of "The Epistle to the Galatians" (Expositor's Bible), pp. 42, 43.*

The warnings of the spirit of prophecy deal with this peril in its many phases, as the following extracts clearly indicate:

Formalism in Preaching

"Scores of men have preached the word when they themselves had not faith in it, and did not obey its teachings. They were unconverted, unsanctified, unholy. But if we would stand the test, piety must be brought into the life. What we want is inspiration from the cross of Calvary. Then God will open eyes to see that we are not to expect to do any work for the Master successfully, unless we connect with Christ. If we are indeed laborers together with God, we shall not have a *dead, scientific religion*, but our hearts will be infused with a living power, even the

72

Spirit of Jesus." *–Review and Herald, Jan. 31, 1893.*

"Many present the doctrines and theories of our faith; but their presentation is as salt without savor; for the Holy Spirit is not working through their faithless ministry. They have not opened the heart to receive the grace of Christ; they know not the operation of the Spirit; they are as meal without leaven; for there is no working principle in all their labor, and they fail to win souls to Christ. They do not appropriate the righteousness of Christ; it is a robe unworn by them, a fullness unknown, a fountain untouched." *–Review and Herald, Nov. 29, 1892.*

"Ministers are wanted who feel the necessity of being laborers together with God, who will go forth to bring the people up in spiritual knowledge to the full measure of Christ. Ministers are wanted who will educate themselves by solemn, reverential communion with God in the closet, so that they shall be men of power in prayer. Piety is degenerating into a dead form, and it is necessary to strengthen the things that remain that are ready to die." *–Review and Herald, May 24, 1892.*

"A man may preach pleasing, entertaining sermons, yet be far from Christ as regard religious experience. He may be exalted to the pinnacle of human greatness, yet never have experienced the inward work of grace that transforms the character. Such a one is deceived by his connection and familiarity with the sacred truths of the gospel, which have reached the intellect, but have not been brought into the inner sanctuary of the soul. We must have more than an intellectual belief in the truth." *–Review and Herald, Feb. 14, 1899.*

"Could we now leave the cold, traditional sentiments which hinder our advancement, we would view the work of saving souls in an altogether different light." *–Review and Herald, May 6, 1890.*

Theory of Truth Is Not Sufficient

"Our doctrines may be correct; we may hate false doctrine, and may not receive those who are not true to principle; we may labor with untiring energy; but even this is not sufficient. . . A belief in the theory of the truth is not enough. To present this theory to unbelievers does not constitute you a witness for Christ." —*Review and Herald, Feb. 3, 1891.*

"The trouble with our work has been that we have been content to present a cold theory of the truth." —*Review and Herald,* May 28, 1889.

"How much more power would attend the preaching of the word today, if men dwelt less upon the theories and arguments of men, and far more upon the lessons of Christ, and upon practical godliness." – *Review and Herald, Jan. 7, 1890.*

The Only Way Truth Becomes of Value to the Soul

"The truth is of no value to any soul unless it is *brought into the inner sanctuary, and sanctifies the soul.* Piety will degenerate, and religion become a shallow sentimentalism, unless the plowshare of truth is made to go deep into the fallow ground of the heart." —*Review and Herald, May 24, 1892.*

"A theoretical knowledge of the truth is essential. But the knowledge of the greatest truth will not save us; our knowledge must be practical. . . *The truth must be brought into their hearts,* sanctifying and cleansing them from all earthliness and sensuality in the most private life. The soul temple must be cleansed." —*Review and Herald, May 24, 1887.*

"The greatest deception of the human mind in Christ's day was, that a mere assent to the truth constituted righteousness. In all human experience a theoretical knowledge of the truth has been proved to be insufficient for the saving of the soul. It does not bring forth the fruits of righteousness. A jealous regard for what is termed theological truth, often accompanies a hatred of genuine truth as made manifest in life. The darkest chapters of history are burdened with the record of crimes committed by bigoted religionists. The Pharisees claimed to be children of Abraham, and boasted of their possession of the oracles of God; yet these advantages did not preserve them from selfishness, malignity, greed for gain, and the basest hypocrisy. They thought themselves the greatest religionists of the world, but their so-called orthodoxy led them to crucify the Lord of glory.

"The same danger still exists. Many take it for granted that they are

Christians, simply because they subscribe to certain theological tenets. But they have not brought the truth into practical life. They have not believed and loved it, therefore they have not received the power and grace that come through sanctification of the truth. Men may profess faith in the truth; but if it does not make them sincere, kind, patient, forbearing, heavenly minded, it is a curse to its possessors, and through their influence it is a curse to the world." –*"The Desire of Ages," pp. 309, 310.*

"The tremendous issues of eternity demand of us something besides an imaginary religion, –a religion of words and form, where the truth is kept in the outer court, to be admired as we admire a beautiful flower; they demand something more than a religion of feeling, which distrusts God when trials and difficulties come. Holiness does not consist in profession, but in lifting the cross, doing the will of God." – *Review and Herald, May 21, 1908.*

"In the lives of many of those whose names are on the church books there has been no genuine change. The truth has been kept in the outer court. There has been no genuine conversion, no positive work of grace done in the heart. Their desire to do God's will is based upon their own inclination, not upon the deep conviction of the Holy Spirit. Their conduct is not brought into harmony with the law of God. They profess to accept Christ as their Saviour, but they do not believe that he will give them power to overcome their sins. They have not a personal acquaintance with a living Saviour, and their characters reveal many blemishes." –*Review and Herald, July 7, 1904.*

"Our hope is to be constantly strengthened by the knowledge that Christ is our righteousness. . . The meager views which so many have had of the exalted character and office of Christ have narrowed their religious experience, and have greatly hindered their progress in the divine life. Personal religion among us as a people is at a low ebb. There is much form, much machinery, much tongue religion; but something deeper and more solid must be brought into our religious experience. . . What we need is to know God and the power of His love, as revealed in Christ, by an experimental knowledge. . . Through the merits of Christ, through His righteousness to the perfection of Christian character." – *"Testimonies," Vol. V, pp. 742-744 (written in 1880).*

Cold, Legal Religion –A Christless Religion

"A cold, legal religion can never lead souls to Christ; for it is a loveless, Christless religion." –*Review and Herald, March 20, 1894.*

"The saving salt is the pure first love, the love of Jesus, the gold tried in the fire. When this is left out of the religious experience, Jesus is not there; the light, the sunshine of His presence, is not there. What, then, is the religion worth? –Just as much as the salt that has lost its savor. It is a *loveless religion.* Then there is an effort to supply the lack by busy activity, a *zeal that is Christless*." –*Review and Herald, Feb. 9, 1892.*

Formal Religion Devoid of Saving Faith

"High pretensions, forms, and ceremonies, however imposing, do not make the heart good and the character pure. True love for God is an active principle, a purifying agency. . .The Jewish nation had occupied the highest position; they had built walls great and high to enclose themselves from association with the heathen world; they had represented themselves as the special, loyal people who were favored of God. But Christ presented their religion as devoid of saving faith." –*Review and Herald, April 30, 1895.*

"It is possible to be a formal, partial believer, and yet be found wanting, and lose eternal life. It is possible to practice some of the Bible injunctions, and be regarded as a Christian, and yet perish because you are lacking in essential qualifications that constitute Christian character."—*Review and Herald, Jan. 11, 1887.*

"To subscribe the name to a church creed is not of the least value to anyone if the heart is not truly changed. . . Men may be church members, and may apparently work earnestly, performing a round of duties from year to year, and yet be unconverted." –*Review and Herald, Feb. 14, 1899.*

"There is a form of religion which is nothing more than selfishness.

It takes pleasure in worldly enjoyment. It is satisfied with contemplating the religion of Christ, and knows nothing of its saving power. Those who possess this religion regard sin lightly because they do not know Jesus. While in this condition they estimate duty very lightly." –*Review and Herald, May 21, 1908.*

"It is painful to see the unbelief that exists in the hearts of many of God's professed followers. We have the most precious truths ever committed to mortals, and the faith of those who have received these truths should correspond to their greatness and value." –*Review and Herald, March 5, 1889.*

"There are many who do not feel averse to suffering, but they do not exercise simple, living faith. They say they do not know what it means to take God at His word. They have a religion of outward forms and observances." –*Review and Herald, March 5, 1889.*

"All who assume the ornaments of the sanctuary, but are not clothed with Christ's righteousness, will appear in the shame of their own nakedness." –*"Testimonies," Vol. V, p. 81.*

"The five foolish virgins had lamps (this means a knowledge of Scripture truth), but they had not the grace of Christ. Day by day they went through a round of ceremonies and external duties, but their service was lifeless, devoid of the righteousness of Christ. The Sun of Righteousness did not shine in their hearts and minds, and they had not the love of the truth which conforms to the life and character, the image and superscription, of Christ. The oil of grace was not mingled with their endeavors. Their religion was a dry husk without the true kernel. They held fast to forms of doctrines, but they were deceived in their Christian life full of self-righteousness, and failing to learn lessons in the school of Christ, which, if practiced, would have made them wise unto salvation." –*Review and Herald, March 27, 1894.*

Danger in Depending Upon Human Plans and Methods

"While we are incased in self-righteousness, and trust in ceremonies, and depend on rigid rules, *we cannot do the work for this time.*" –*Review and Herald, May 6, 1890.*

"The observance of external forms will never meet the great want of the human soul. A mere profession of Christ is not enough to prepare one to stand the test of the judgment." –*Review and Herald, Jan. 25, 1887.*

"Let us not forget that as activity increases, and we become successful in doing the work that must be accomplished, there is danger of our trusting in human plans and methods. There will be a tendency to pray less, and to have less faith."—*Review and Herald, July 4, 1893.*

"Spiritual things have not been discerned. Appearance and machinery have been exalted as of power, while the virtues of true goodness, noble piety, and heart-holiness, have been made a secondary consideration. That which should have been made first has been made last and of least importance." –*Review and Herald, Feb. 27. 1894.*

"When fasting and prayers are practiced in a self-justifying spirit, they are abominable to God. The solemn assembly for worship, the round of religious ceremonies, the external humiliation, the imposed sacrifice, –all proclaim to the world the testimony that the doer of these things considers himself righteous. These things call attention to the observer of rigorous duties, saying, This man is entitled to heaven. But it is all a deception. Works will not buy for us an entrance into heaven. . . Faith in Christ will be the means whereby the right spirit and motive will actuate the believer, and all goodness and heavenly mindedness will proceed from him who looks unto Jesus, the author and finisher of his faith." –*Review and Herald, March 20, 1894.*

"There are many who seem to imagine that outside observances are sufficient for salvation; but formalism, rigorous attendance on religious exercises, will fail to bring the peace of God which passeth understanding. It is Jesus alone who can give us peace." –*Review and Herald, Nov. 18, 1890.*

"Those who have not a daily experience in the things of God will not move wisely. They may have a legal religion, a form of godliness, there may be an appearance of light in the church; all the machinery— much of it human invention—may appear to be working well, and yet the church may be as destitute of the grace of God as were the hills of Gilboa of dew and rain." –*Review and Herald, Jan. 31, 1893.*

Chapter Nine

The Great Truth Lost Sight Of

That such a fundamental, all-embracing truth as imputed righteousness—justification by faith—should be lost sight of by many professing godliness and entrusted with heaven's final message to a dying world, seems incredulous; but such, we are plainly told, is a fact.

"The doctrine of justification by faith has been lost sight of by many who have professed to believe the third angel's message."–*Review and Herald, Aug. 13, 1889.*

"There is not one in one hundred who understands for himself the Bible truth on this subject [justification by faith] that is so necessary to our present and eternal welfare." –*Review and Herald, Sept. 3, 1889.*

"For the last twenty years a subtle, unconsecrated influence has been leading men to look to men, to bind up with men, to neglect their heavenly Companion. Many have turned away from Christ. They have failed to appreciate the One who declares, Lo, I am with you always, even unto the end of the world.' Let us do all in our power to redeem the past."–*Review and Herald, Feb. 18, 1904.*

Twenty years back from 1904 would just take in the sweep of the message of Righteousness by Faith in 1888, with the preparatory messages which immediately preceded it. What do you say, fellow workers? Shall we not do all in our power to redeem the past? It may be that in returning from the feast we have left Jesus behind, and it becomes necessary for us to seek Him sorrowing, as did Joseph and Mary on their journey homeward from Jerusalem. We are told that—

"The reason why our preachers accomplish so little is that they do not walk with God. He is a day's journey from most of them."–*"Testimonies for the Church," Vol. I, p. 434.*

It is an individual matter. Let us pause and consider: is the Saviour a living, abiding presence in my life? Or is He a day's journey distant, and my life and work the result of the *memory* of His presence?

The searching warning sent through the spirit of prophecy regarding the large number of Seventh-day Adventists who had lost sight of the "doctrine of justification by faith," was written in 1889. What change time has made in the proportion of our people who did not at that time hold to or understand this precious truth, none will attempt to say; but we do know that every believer in the third angel's message at this time should have a clear conception of the doctrine of justification by faith and a well-grounded experience in the great transaction.

What It Means to Lose Sight of Such a Truth

To lose sight of this precious truth of justification by faith is to miss the supreme purpose of the gospel, which must prove disastrous to the individual, no matter how well meaning and earnest he may be regarding doctrines, ceremonies, activities, and anything and everything else relating to religion. The warning is clearly given by the servant of the Lord:

"Unless *divine power is brought into the experience* of the people of God, false theories and erroneous ideas will take minds captive, Christ and His righteousness will be dropped out of the experience of many, and their faith will be without power or life. Such will not have a daily living experience of the love of God in the heart; and if they do not zealously repent, they will be among those who are represented by the Laodiceans, who will be spewed out of the mouth of God." –*Review and Herald, Sept. 3, 1889.*

To a lamentable degree, God's people failed to bring the divine power into their experience, and the result predicted has been seen:

1. False theories and erroneous ideas have taken minds captive.

80

2. Christ and His righteousness have been dropped out of the experience of many.

3. The faith of many is without power or life.

4. There is not a living daily experience of the love of God in the heart.

Still further, we are told that much has been lost to the cause of God by the failure to gain that living experience of divine power, – righteousness by faith:

"The people of God have lost much by not maintaining the simplicity of the truth as it is in Jesus. This simplicity has been crowded out, and forms and ceremonies and a round of busy activities in mechanical work have taken its place. Pride and lukewarmness have made the professed people of God an offense in His sight. Boastful self-sufficiency and complacent self-righteousness have masked and concealed the beggary and nakedness of the soul; but with God all things are naked and manifest.'–*Review and Herald, Aug. 7, 1894.*

Thus has been brought about widespread and fatal deception:

"What is it that constitutes the wretchedness, the nakedness, of those who feel rich and increased with goods? It is the want of the righteousness of Christ. In their own righteousness they are represented as clothed with filthy rags, and yet in this condition they flatter themselves that they are clothed upon with Christ's righteousness. Could deception be greater?" –*Review and Herald, Aug. 7, 1894.*

Martin Luther Feared This Great Truth Would Become Defaced

The fear that the doctrine of justification by faith, –so dear to his heart and through which the great Reformation was brought about– would be lost sight of, seems to have been dominant in the mind of Luther as he caught a vision of future events to transpire in the world. We read:

"If the article of justification be once lost, then is all true Christian doctrine lost. . . He then that strayeth from this 'Christian righteousness,' must needs fall into the 'righteousness of the law;' that is to say, when he hath lost Christ, he must fall into the confidence of his own works." "For if we *neglect* the article of justification, we *lose it altogether*. Therefore most necessary it is, chiefly, and above all things, that we teach and repeat this article continually." "Yea, though we learn it and understand it well, yet is there none that taketh hold of it perfectly, or believeth it with his heart." "Therefore I fear lest this doctrine will be defaced and darkened again, when we are dead. For the world must be replenished with horrible darkness and errors, before the latter day come." *—"Luther on Galatians," pp. 136, 148, 149, 402.*

As God called Luther from the midnight darkness of the sixteenth century, and placed in his hands this torch of truth—"THE JUST SHALL LIVE BY FAITH," so will God ever have His standard-bearers to uphold this fundamental basis of salvation in connection with "present truth" in the various stages of the proclamation of the last gospel message in all the world. It is therefore timely that we, today, give this vital truth most earnest, thorough study. It should be just as clearly understood as to how a sinner may be transformed into a saint, as we have been taught to understand how Adam, a sinless man, became a sinner. Justification by faith should be as clear to our minds as the teaching regarding the law, the Sabbath, the coming of the Lord, and every other doctrine revealed in the Scriptures. But it is not so understood by many; and because it is neither appreciated nor experienced as it should be, there is failure on the part of such to present it in their teaching. This failure was recognized and clearly pointed out back in 1889, for we read:

"The Ministers have not presented Christ in His fullness to the people, either in the churches or in new fields, and the people have not an intelligent faith. They have not been instructed as they should have been, that Christ is unto them both salvation and righteousness."*—Review and Herald, Sept. 3, 1889.*

Duty of Minsters to Present the Message of Righteousness by Faith

The following paragraphs furnish most excellent and appropriate counsel to ministers and other gospel workers, while clearly pointing out the sad fact that the center of attraction, Jesus, has been made secondary by many, while theories and arguments have been given first place. What a fatal mistake!

"Laborers in the cause of truth should present the righteousness of Christ, not as new light, but as precious light that has for a time been lost sight of by the people. We are to accept Christ as our personal Saviour, and He imputes unto us the righteousness of God in Christ.'–*Review and Herald, March 20, 1894.*

"Do not allow your minds to be diverted from the all-important theme of the righteousness of Christ by the study of theories. Do not imagine that the performance of ceremonies, the observance of outward forms, will make you an heir of heaven. We want to keep the mind steadfastly to the point for which we are working; for it is now the day of the Lord's preparation, and we should yield our hearts to God, that they may be softened and subdued by the Holy Spirit."–*Review and Herald, April 5, 1892.*

"The great center of attraction, Jesus Christ, must not be left out of the third angel's message. By many who have been engaged in the work for this time, Christ has been made secondary, and theories and arguments have had the first place."–*Review and Herald, March 20, 1894*

"The mystery of the incarnation of Christ, the account of His sufferings, His crucifixion, His resurrection, and His ascension, open to all humanity the marvelous love of God. This imparts a power to the truth."–*Review and Herald, June 18, 1895.*

"The small churches have been presented to me as so destitute of spiritual food that they are ready to die, and God says to you, 'Be watchful, and strengthen the things which remain, that are ready to die; for I have not found thy works perfect before God.'"–*Review and Herald, March 4, 1890.*

"This I do know, that our churches are dying for the want of teaching on the subject of righteousness by faith in Christ, and on kindred truths."–*"Gospel Workers," p. 301.*

"The theme that attracts the heart of the sinner is Christ and Him crucified. On the cross of Calvary, Jesus stands revealed to the world in unparalleled love. Present Him thus to the hungering multitudes, and the light of His love will win men from darkness to light, from transgression to obedience and true holiness. Beholding Jesus upon the cross of Calvary arouses the conscience to the heinous character of sin as nothing else can do."–*Review and Herald, Nov. 22, 1892.*

"Christ crucified–talk it, pray it, sing it, and it will break and win hearts. Set, formal phrases, the presentation of merely argumentative subjects, is productive of little good. The melting love of God in the hearts of the workers will be recognized by those for whom they labor. Souls are thirsting for the water of life. Do not allow them to go from you empty. Reveal the love of Christ to them. Lead them to Jesus, and He will give them the bread of life and the water of salvation."–*Review and Herald, June 2, 1903.*

This chapter may be fittingly closed by the following peerless statement, which sums up the burden of the message of the spirit of prophecy and gives us the clue to the line of our investigation:

"If through the grace of Christ His people will become new bottles, he will fill them with the new wine. God will give additional light, and old truths will be recovered, and replaced in the framework of truth; and wherever the laborers go, they will triumph. As Christ's ambassadors, they are to search the Scriptures, to seek for the truths that have been hidden beneath the rubbish of error. And every ray of light received is to be communicated to others. One interest will prevail, one subject will swallow up every other, –*CHRIST OUR RIGHTEOUSNESS.*"–*Review and Herald, Extra, Dec. 23, 1890.*

Chapter Ten

Restoration Full and Complete Provided

When the sinner enters through the door of faith into the new life in Christ Jesus, he finds that not only has he been pardoned for transgression of the law, but restoration full and complete is provided. Furthermore, provision is made in Christ for the maintenance of that which has been restored. He enters upon a new and higher plane of life, in harmony with the following direction and assurance:

"We must unite with Christ. There is a reservoir of power at our command, and *we are not to remain in the dark, cold, sunless cave of unbelief,* or we shall not catch the bright beams of the Sun of Righteousness."–*Review and Herald, Jan. 24, 1893.*

"We must *rise above the frosty atmosphere* in which we have hitherto lived, and with which Satan would surround our souls, and breathe in the hallowed atmosphere of heaven."—*Review and Herald, May 6, 1890.*

The whole story of redemption and restoration is clearly set forth in the following beautiful statement by the pen of inspiration:

"Through Christ, restoration as well as reconciliation is provided for man.

"The gulf that was made by sin has been spanned by the cross of Calvary.

"A full, complete ransom has been paid by Jesus, by virtue of which the sinner is pardoned, and the justice of the law is maintained.

"All who believe that Christ is the atoning sacrifice may come and

85

receive pardon for their sins; for through the merit of Christ communication has been opened between God and man.

"God can accept me as His child, and I can claim Him and rejoice in Him as my loving Father.

"We must center our hopes of heaven upon Christ alone, because he is our substitute and surety.

"We have transgressed the law of God, and by the deeds of the law shall no flesh be justified. The best efforts that man in his own strength can make, are valueless to meet the holy and just law that he has transgressed; but through faith in Christ he may claim the righteousness of the Son of God as all-sufficient.

"Christ satisfied the demands of the law in His human nature.

"He bore the curse of the law for the sinner, made an atonement for him, that whosoever believeth in Him should not perish, but have everlasting life.

"Genuine faith appropriates the righteousness of Christ, and the sinner is made an overcomer with Christ; for he is made a partaker of the divine nature, and thus divinity and humanity are combined.

"He who is trying to reach heaven by his own works in keeping the law, is attempting an impossibility.

"Men cannot be saved without obedience, but his works should not be of himself; Christ should work in him to will and to do of His good pleasure."—*Review and Herald, July 1, 1890.*

Let us carefully review this message which unfolds to the human mind the sublimest facts of the gospel of our Lord and Saviour Jesus Christ:

> 1. Restoration full and complete is provided for sinners. The atoning sacrifice of Christ on the cross not only made our *reconciliation* with God possible, but it also made possible, for every sinner who may choose to accept the offer, *restoration* to Adam's glorious standing before he sinned.
>
> 2. The great gulf made by sin, that separates us so far from God

and heaven, has been spanned by the cross of Calvary. What cause for praise and adoration!

3. The great problem of pardoning the sinner and at the same time maintaining the justice of God's holy law, has been solved. Christ became our substitute. He took our place, and thus ransomed us from condemnation and death.

4. By His atoning sacrifice, Christ opened communication between God and poor, sinful, lost man, so that we can now come to Him and receive pardon, cleansing, and salvation from all sin.

5. Because Christ alone became our substitute and surety, all our hopes center in Him. There is no other name, no other way.

6. Because of man's transgression of the law, no flesh can ever be justified by the deeds of the law. But through faith in Christ, man may claim the righteousness of Christ as all-sufficient.

7. By appropriating the righteousness of Christ by faith, we are made overcomers with Christ, and thus become partakers of the divine nature.

8. In trying to reach heaven by the works of the law, we are attempting an utter impossibility.

9. While we cannot be saved without obedience, that obedience cannot be of ourselves. It must be Christ's obedience working in and through us, causing us to will and to do of His good pleasure.

Imputed, Then Imparted Righteousness

Righteousness by faith in all its meaning, is comprehended in the following definition:

"The righteousness by which we are *justified* is *imputed*. The righteousness by which we are *sanctified* is *imparted*. The first is our *title to heaven*; the second is our *fitness for heaven*"–*Review and Herald, June 4, 1895.*

Imputed righteousness, by which man is justified from guilt, is the foundation upon which imparted righteousness is bestowed, which sanctifies the life conduct, and provides "our fitness for heaven." As to the operation of these living principles, we quote as follows:

"Christ has become our sacrifice and surety. He has become sin for us, that we might become the righteousness of God in Him. Through faith in his name, He imputes unto us His righteousness, and it becomes a living principle in our life."–*Review and Herald, July 12, 1892.*

"No repentance is genuine that does not work reformation. The righteousness of Christ is not a cloak to cover unconfessed and unforsaken sin; it is a principle of life that transform the character and controls the conduct. Holiness is wholeness for God; it is the entire surrender of heart and life to the indwelling of the principles of heaven"–*"The Desire of Ages," p. 555, 637.*

"Christ imputes to us His sinless character and presents us to the Father in His own purity. There are many who think that it is impossible to escape from the power of sin, but the promise is that we may be filled with all the fullness of God. We aim too low. The mark is much higher."–*Review and Herald, July 12, 1892.*

"Jesus is our great High Priest in heaven. And what is He doing? He is making intercession and atonement for his people who believe in him. Through His imputed righteousness, they are accepted of God as those who are manifesting to the world that they acknowledge allegiance to God, keeping all His commandments."–*Review and Herald, Aug. 22, 1893.*

"In the religion of Christ there is a regenerating influence that transforms the entire being, lifting man above every debasing, groveling vice, and raising the thoughts and desires toward God and heaven. Linked to the Infinite One, man is made partaker of the divine nature. Upon him the shafts of evil have no effect; for his is clothed with the *panoply of Christ's righteousness.*"–*"Counsels to Teachers," pp. 51, 52.*

"When the soul surrenders itself to Christ, a new power takes possession of the new heart. A change is wrought which man can never accomplish for himself. It is a supernatural work, bringing a supernatural element into human nature. The soul that is yielded to Christ, becomes His own fortress, which he holds in a revolted world, and he intends that no authority shall be known in it but His own. A soul thus kept in possession by the heavenly agencies, is impregnable to the assaults of Satan. But unless we do yield ourselves to the control of Christ, we shall be dominated by the wicked one. We must inevitably be under the control of the one or the other of the two great powers that are contending for the supremacy of the world.

"It is not necessary for us deliberately to choose the service of the kingdom of darkness in order to come under its dominion. We have only to neglect to ally ourselves with the kingdom of light. If we do not cooperate with the heavenly agencies, Satan will take possession of the heart, and will make it his abiding place. The only defense against evil is the indwelling of Christ in the heart through faith in His righteousness. Unless we become vitally connected with God, we can never resist the unhallowed effects of self-love, self-indulgence, and temptation to sin. We may leave off many bad habits, for the time we may part company with Satan; but without a vital connection with God, through the surrender of ourselves to Him moment by moment, we shall be overcome. Without a personal acquaintance with Christ, and a continual communion, we are at the mercy of the enemy, and shall do his bidding in the end."–*"The Desire of Ages," pp. 323, 324.*

The Outward Evidence of the Indwelling Righteousness

"Righteousness within is testified to by righteousness without. He who is righteous within is not hardhearted and unsympathetic, but day by day he grows into the image of Christ, going on from strength to strength. He who is being sanctified by the truth will be self-controlled, and will follow in the footsteps of Christ until grace is lost in glory."–*Review and Herald, June 4, 1895.*

"When we accept Christ, good works will appear as fruitful evidence that we are in the way of life, that Christ is our way, and that we are treading the true path that leads to heaven."–*Review and Herald, Nov. 4, 1890.*

"When we are clothed with the righteousness of Christ, we shall *have no relish for sin*; for Christ will be working with us. We may make mistakes, but we will hate the sin that caused the sufferings of the Son of God."–*Review and Herald, March 18, 1890.*

"When Christ is in the heart, it will be so softened and subdued by love for God and man that fretting, faultfinding, and contention will not exist there. The religion of Christ in the heart will gain for its possessor a complete victory over those passions that are seeking for the mastery."–*"Testimonies for the Church," Vol. IV, page 610.*

"When a man is converted to God, a *new moral taste* is created; and he loves the things that God loves; for his life is bound up by the golden chain of the immutable promises, to the life of Jesus. His heart is drawn out after God. His prayer is, 'Open Thou mine eyes, that I many behold wondrous things out of Thy law.' In the immutable standard he sees the character of the Redeemer, and knows that though he has sinned, he is not to be saved *in* his sins; but *from* his sins; for Jesus is the Lamb of God which taketh away the sin of the world." –*Review and Herald, June 21, 1892.*

Thus it is clear that "man cannot be saved without obedience, but his works should not be of himself; *Christ should work in him* to will and to do of His good pleasure." Christ becomes not only the "author," but the "finisher" of our faith.

"As we near the close of time, the current of evil will set more and more decidedly toward perdition. We can be safe only as we hold firmly to the hand of Jesus, constantly looking to the Author and Finisher of our faith. He is our mighty helper."–*Review and Herald, Oct. 7, 1890.*

Wearing the Spotless Robe of Righteousness

Although the righteousness of Christ is freely offered, and provides restoration full and complete for the sinner; yet we are told that some "*do not appropriate* the righteousness of Christ; it is a robe unworn by them, a fullness unknown, a fountain untouched." How can there be such failure to accept and appropriate this greatest of all gifts, when—

"Only those who are clothed in the garments of His righteousness will be able to endure the glory of His presence when He shall appear with 'power and great glory.'"–*Review and Herald, July 9, 1908.*

"On Christ's coronation day, He will not acknowledge as His any who wear spot or wrinkle or any such thing. But to His faithful ones He will give crowns of immortal glory. Those who would not that He should reign over them will see Him surrounded by the army of the redeemed, each of whom bears the sign, 'THE LORD OUR RIGHTEOUSNESS.'" –*Review and Herald, Nov. 24, 1904.*

Chapter Eleven

Entering Into the Experience

In considering the phase of entering into the experience of being justified by faith, it is helpful to note the direct question and the positive answer which are on record concerning the experience.

"*What is justification by faith?* It is the work of God in laying the glory of man in the dust, and doing for man that which it is not in his power to do for himself. When men see their own nothingness, they are prepared to be clothed with the righteousness of Christ."–*Review and Herald, Sept. 16, 1902.*

This experience of being justified, or accounted righteous, is an individual matter between the soul and God. It cannot be received by proxy. There is only one door of entrance into this experience,–

The Door of Faith

"Faith is the condition upon which God has seen fit to promise pardon to sinners: not that there is any virtue in faith whereby salvation is merited, but because faith can lay hold of the merits of Christ, the remedy provided for sin."—*Review and Herald, Nov. 4, 1890.*

"When we are clothed with the righteousness of Christ, we shall have no relish for sin; for Christ will be working with us. . . A door has been opened, and no man can close it, neither the highest powers nor the lowest; you alone can close the door of your heart, so that the Lord cannot reach you."–*Review and Herald, March 18, 1890.*

Close beside this *door* of faith, the enemy of all righteousness has placed another door, a broader and more conspicuous entrance,–

The Door of Works

Through this door many pilgrims bound for the heavenly Canaan unconsciously enter upon the path which ends in destruction, and sooner or later find that the beautiful garments of self-righteousness have become "filthy rags," entirely unfit to appear in the presence of the King. Of this class it is said:

"Many are losing the right way in consequence of thinking that they must climb to heaven, that they must do something to merit the favor of God. They seek to make themselves better by their own unaided efforts. This they can never accomplish. Christ has made the way by dying our sacrifice, by living our example by becoming our great high priest. He declares, 'I am the way, the truth, and the life.' If by any efforts of our own we could advance one step toward the ladder, the words of Christ would not be true."–*Review and Herald, Nov. 4, 1890.*

"There are many who seem to feel that they have a great work to do themselves before they can come to Christ for his salvation. They seem to think that Jesus will come in at the very last of their struggle, and give them help by putting the finishing touch to their life-work. It seems difficult for them to understand that Christ is a complete Saviour, and able to save to the uttermost all that come unto God by Him. They lose sight of the fact that Christ Himself is 'the way, the truth, and the life.'"–*Review and Herald, March 5, 1889.*

May the Lord help us all to enter through the right door and be filled with the righteousness of Christ! For each soul there must be performed "the work of God in laying the glory of man in the dust, and doing for man that which it is not in his power to do for himself."

Realization of Hopeless Condition

But first of all, in entering into this experience, man must be brought to a realization of his hopeless condition; and this is accomplished "through the impartation of the grace of Christ."

"Without the grace of Christ, the sinner is in a hopeless condition; nothing can be done for him; but through divine grace, supernatural power is imparted to the man, and works in mind and heart and character. It is through the impartation of the grace of Christ that sin is discerned in its hateful nature, and finally driven from the soul-temple. It is through grace that we are brought into fellowship with Christ, to be associated with Him in the work of salvation."–*Review and Herald, Nov. 4, 1890.*

"Without the grace of Christ, the sinner is in a hopeless condition; nothing can be done for him." That is, the sinner cannot clear himself. Nor can any other sinner help him. The law which he has transgressed cannot pardon nor pass over his sin; nor can anything in this world be found which will furnish deliverance. But "through divine grace, supernatural power is imparted to the man, and works in mind and heart and character." How illuminating and assuring is this word to the sinner! Through divine grace, through the great mercy and compassion of God, provision has been made for imparting "supernatural power" to the hopeless sinner.

But what is "supernatural power"? It is a power far above and beyond anything that resides in man. It is beyond anything that man can lay hold of in this world. It is that "all power . . in heaven and in earth" that Christ declared was given unto Him, –that supernatural power by which all His miracles were wrought during his ministry on earth.

Concerning that "supernatural power," the following statement by Dr. Philip Schaff is worthy of consideration:

"All His [Christ's] miracles are but the *natural* manifestations of His person, and hence they were performed with the *same ease with which we perform our ordinary daily works.* . . . The supernatural and miraculous element in Christ, let it be borne in mind, was not a borrowed gift or an occasional manifestation. . . An inward virtue dwelt in His person, and

94

went forth from Him, so that even the fringe of His garment was healing to the touch through the medium of faith, which is the bond of union between Him and the soul."–*"The Person of Christ," pp. 76, 77.*

It is the same supernatural power that Christ imparts to man, and
which *works* in the mind, the heart, and the character.

Now mark the wonderful results, as stated in the further quotation
from the spirit of prophecy: "It is through the impartation of the grace
of Christ that sin is discerned in its hateful nature, and finally driven
from the soul-temple. It is through grace that we are brought into fellowship with Christ, to be associated with Him in the work of salvation." Thus we see that the "supernatural power" imparted to man
through the grace of Christ, works in his mind and his heart, revealing
to him the hateful nature of sin and leading him to permit that corrupt-
ing thing to be driven from the soul-temple.

The Consent and Choice of the Sinner

But this marvelous work wrought in the heart by the supernatural
power of Christ is not done without the consent and choice of the sinner. Note the following:

"Faith is the condition upon which God has seen fit to promise
pardon to sinners; not that there is any virtue in faith whereby salvation
is merited, but because faith can lay hold of the merits of Christ, the
remedy provided for sin. Faith can present Christ's perfect obedience
instead of the sinner's transgression and defection. When the sinner
believes that Christ is his personal Saviour, then, according to His unfailing promises, God pardons his sin, and justifies him freely. The repentant soul realizes that his justification comes because Christ, as his
substitute and surety, has died for him, is his atonement and righteousness."–*Review and Herald, Nov. 4, 1890.*

The exercise of faith is our part in the great transaction by which
sinners are changed to saints. But we must remember there is no virtue
in the faith we exercise. "whereby salvation is merited." That is to say,
there is no virtue in faith itself, nor in the act of exercising it. The virtue
is all in Christ. He is the remedy provided for sin. Faith is the act by

95

which the ruined, helpless, doomed sinner lays hold of the remedy. "Faith can present Christ's perfect obedience instead of the sinner's transgression and defection." This is truly a sublime thought! It is that marvelous science of redemption in which the saints will rejoice through eternity, yet it is so simple in its operation that the weakest and most unworthy can enter into it in all its meaning and fullness.

Living Faith Accompanied by Action

Entering through the door of faith into the fullness of imputed and imparted righteousness, involves more than a mere mental assent to the provisions laid down. It is the archway of "living faith, that works by love and purifies the soul." In order to pass this portal, there must be compliance with certain requirements:

1. *There must cease to be practice of all known sin, and no longer neglect of known duty.*

   "But while God can be just, and yet justify the sinner through the merits of Christ, no man can cover his soul with the garments of Christ's righteousness while practicing known sins or neglecting known duties. God requires the entire surrender of the heart, before justification can take place; and in order for man to retain justification, there must be continual obedience, through active, living faith that works by love and purifies the soul." *—Review and Herald, Nov. 4, 1890.*

2. *Willingness to pay the price —give up all.*

   "The righteousness of Christ, as a pure white pearl, has no defect, no stain, no guilt. This righteousness may be ours. Salvation, with its blood-bought, inestimable treasures, is the pearl of great price. It may be searched for and found. . . In the parable the merchantman is represented as selling all that he had to gain possession of one pearl of great price. This is a beautiful representation of those who appreciate the truth so highly that they *give up all they have* to come into possession of it." *—Review and Herald, Aug. 8, 1899.*

96

3. *Entire surrender of wrong habits.*

"There are some who are seeking, always seeking, for the goodly pearl. But they do not make an entire surrender of their wrong habits. They do not die to self that Christ may live in them. Therefore they do not find the precious pearl." –*Review and Herald, Aug. 8, 1899.*

4. *The will power placed in cooperation with God.*

"The Lord does not design that human power should be paralyzed; but by cooperating with God, the power of man may be efficient for good. God does not design that our will should be destroyed; for it is through this very attribute that we are to accomplish the work He would have us to do both at home and abroad."–*Review and Herald, Nov., 1892.*

How sincerely and earnestly we should follow this clear instruction, and enter fully into the experience of being accounted and made righteous, justified, and sanctified through faith in Christ! How deeply and keenly we should realize our hopeless condition, so far as we can do anything of ourselves! It is only through the grace of God that we can be delivered. How we should cherish the great truth that through divine grace, supernatural power may be imparted to us! We should accept at full value the assurance that sin in all its hatefulness can be driven from the soul-temple. We should realize that our part in this great transaction is to choose and accept it by faith, when we have fully complied with the conditions. And every day that comes and goes we should humbly plead before the throne of grace the merits, the perfect obedience, of Christ in the place of our transgressions and sins. And in doing this, we should believe and realize that our justification comes through Christ as our substitute and surety, that He has died for us, and He is our atonement and righteousness.

If, on our part, this instruction is followed sincerely and wholeheartedly, God will make the results real in our lives; and "therefore being justified by faith, we have peace with God." Rom. 5:1. We shall experience the joy of salvation, and day by day we shall *know the reality* of victory that overcomes the world, even our faith.

Let us not rest until we have fully entered through the door of faith into that blessed experience of pardon, justification, righteousness, and peace in Christ.

APPENDIX

Additional Gems

"Christians are Christ's jewels. They are to shine brightly for Him, shedding forth the light of His loveliness. Their luster depends on the polishing they receive. They may choose to be polished or to remain unpolished. But everyone who is pronounced worthy of a place in the Lord's temple must submit to the polishing process. Without the polishing that the Lord gives they can reflect no more light than a common pebble. . . .

"The divine Worker spends little time on worthless material. Only the precious jewels does He polish after the similitude of a palace, cutting away all the rough edges. This process is severe and trying; it hurts human pride. Christ cuts deep into the experience that man in his self-sufficiency has regarded as complete, and taken away self-uplifting from the character. He cuts away the surplus surface, and putting the stone to the polishing wheel, presses it close, that all roughness may be worn away. Then, holding the jewel up to the light, the Master sees in it a reflection of Himself, and He pronounces it worthy of a place in His casket." —*Review and Herald, Dec. 19, 1907*

APPENDIX

Gems of Thought

(Miscellaneous Items Not included in Foregoing Chapters)

Christ the Source of Every Right Impulse

Christ Revealed by God the Father

"God reveals Christ to the sinner, and when he sees the purity of the son of God, he is not ignorant of the character of sin. By faith in the work and power of Christ, enmity against sin and Satan is created in his heart. Those whom God pardons are first made penitent."–*Review and Herald, April 1, 1890.*

Christ Draws the Sinner to Himself

"Christ draws the sinner by the exhibition of His love upon the cross, and this softens the heart, impresses the mind, and inspires contrition and repentance in the soul."–*Review and Herald, April 1, 1890.*

"Christ is constantly drawing men to Himself, while Satan is as diligently seeking every imaginable device, to draw men away from their Redeemer."–*Review and Herald, April 1, 1890.*

"As Christ draws them to look upon His cross, to behold Him whom their sins have pierced, the commandment comes home to the conscience. The wickedness of their life, the deep-seated sin of the soul, is revealed to them. They begin to comprehend something of the righteousness of Christ, and exclaim, 'What is sin, that it should require such a sacrifice for the redemption of its victim? Was all this love, all this suffering, all this humiliation, demanded, that we might not perish, but have everlasting life?'"–*Steps to Christ,"p. 31.*

Christ Gives Repentance

"Repentance is as much the gift of Christ as is forgiveness, and it cannot be found in the heart where Jesus has not been at work. We can no more repent without the Spirit of Christ to awaken the conscience than we can be pardoned without Christ." –*Review and Herald, April 1, 1890.*

Christ the Source of Power

"Christ is the source of every right impulse. He is the only one who can arouse in the natural heart enmity against sin. He is the source of our power if we would be saved. No soul can repent without the grace of Christ."–*Review and Herald, April 1, 1890.*

Christ the Embodiment of Righteousness

"The righteousness of God is embodied in Christ. We receive righteousness by receiving Him." –*"Thoughts From the Mount of Blessing," p. 34.*

Christ the Heavenly Merchantman

"Jesus is going from door to door, standing in front of every soul-temple, proclaiming, 'I stand at the door, and knock.' As a heavenly Merchantman, He opens His treasures, and cried, 'Buy of Me gold tried in the fire, that thou mayest be rich; and white raiment that thou mayest be clothed, and that the shame of thy nakedness do not appear.' The gold that He offers is without alloy, more precious than that of Ophir; for it is faith and love. The white raiment he invites the soul to wear is His own robe of righteousness; and the oil for anointing is the oil of His grace, which will give spiritual eyesight to the soul in blindness and darkness, that he may distinguish between the workings of the Spirit of God and the spirit of the enemy. Open your doors, says the great merchantman, the possessor of spiritual riches, and transact your business with me. It is I, your Redeemer, who counsels you to buy of Me." – *Review and Herald, Aug. 7, 1894.*

"The Lord knocks at the door of your heart, desiring to enter, that He may impart spiritual riches to your soul. He would anoint the blind eyes, that they may discover the holy character of God in His law, and understand the love of Christ, which is indeed gold tried in the fire."– *Review and Herald, Feb. 25, 1890.*

The Root of Righteousness

Righteousness has its root in godliness. No man can steadily maintain before his fellow men a pure, forceful life, unless his life is hid with Christ in God. The greater the activity among men, the closer must be the communion of the heart with heaven." –*"The Ministry of Healing," p. 136.*

"Righteousness has its root in godliness. No human being is righteous any longer than he has faith in God and maintains a vital connection with him. As a flower of the field has its root in the soil; as it must receive air, dew, showers, and sunshine, so must we receive from God that which ministers to the life of the soul. It is only through becoming partakers of His nature that we receive power to obey His commandments. No man, high or low, experienced or inexperienced, can steadily maintain before his fellow men a pure, forceful life, unless his life is hid with Christ in God. The greater the activity among men, the closer should be the communion of the heart with God."–*"Testimonies," Vol. VII. P. 194.*

Working Out What Divine Grace Works In

"Because he [man] needs divine aid, it does not make human activity unessential. Faith on the part of man is required; for faith works by love and purifies the soul. . . He has given to every man his work; and every true worker sheds forth light to the world, because he is united with God, and Christ and heavenly angels in the grand work of saving the lost. From divine association he becomes more and more intelligent in working the works of God. In working out what divine grace works in, the believer becomes spiritually great."–*Review and Herald, Nov. 1, 1892.*

The Antidote for Formalism

"The righteousness which Christ taught is conformity of heart and life to the revealed will of God. Sinful men can become righteous only as they have faith in God, and maintain a vital connection with Him. Then true godliness will elevate the thoughts and ennoble the life. Then the external forms of religion accord with the Christian's internal purity. Then the ceremonies required in the service of God are not meaningless rites, like those of the hypocritical Pharisees."–*"The Desire of Ages," p. 310.*

A Power Outside of Man

"In order to gain the victory over every besetment of the enemy, we must lay hold on a power that is out of and beyond ourselves. We must maintain a constant, living connection with Christ, who has power to give victory to every soul that will maintain an attitude of faith and humility."–*Review and Herald, July 8, 1892.*

"Man needs a power out of and above himself to restore him to the likeness of God."–*Review and Herald, Nov. 1, 1892.*

That Power Is Christ

"Faith lays hold upon the virtue of Christ."–*Review and Herald, Nov. 1, 1892.*

Encouragement for the Faint-Hearted

"All who have a sense of their deep soul poverty, who feel that they have nothing good in themselves, may find righteousness and strength by looking unto Jesus. . . He bids you exchange your poverty for the riches of His grace. . . . Whatever may have been your past experience, however discouraging your present circumstances, if you will come to Jesus just as you are, weak, helpless, and despairing, our compassionate Saviour will meet you a great way off, and will throw about you His arms of love and His robe of righteousness."–*"Thoughts from the Mount of Blessing." p. 21.*

Worldly Interests Subordinate

"In order to accept the invitation to the gospel feast, they must make their worldly interests subordinate to the one purpose of receiving Christ and His righteousness. God gave all for man, and He asks him to place His service above every earthly and selfish consideration. He cannot accept a divided heart. The heart that is absorbed in earthly affections cannot be given up to God."–*"Christ's Object Lessons," p. 233.*

"We are to engage in no business, follow no pursuit, seek no pleasure, that would hinder the outworking of His righteousness in our character and life. Whatever we do, is to be done heartily, as unto the Lord."–*"Thoughts from the Mount of Blessing," page 148.*

Timely Themes for Study

The Mediatorial Work of Christ

"The mediatorial work of Christ, the grand and holy mysteries of redemption, are not studied or comprehended by the people who claim to have light in advance of every other people on the face of the earth. Were Jesus personally upon earth, He would address a large number who claim to believe present truth with the words He addressed to the Pharisees: 'ye do err, not knowing the Scriptures, nor the power of God.'"–*Review and Herald, Feb. 4, 1890.*

The Plan of Salvation

As we near the close of time, . . we should devote ourselves to the study of the plan of salvation, that we may have an appreciation of how highly Jehovah has valued the salvation of man."–*Review and Herald, Oct. 7, 1890.*

Faith

"There are old, yet new truths still to be added to the treasures of our knowledge. We do not understand or exercise faith as we should. Christ has made rich promises in regard to bestowing the Holy Spirit upon His church, and yet how little these promises are appreciated! We are not called to worship and serve God by the use of the means employed in former years. God requires higher service now than ever before. He requires the improvement of the heavenly gifts. He has brought us into a position where we need higher and better things than have ever been needed before."–*Review and Herald, Feb. 25, 1890.*

The Law of God in Relation to Righteousness by Faith

The Law the Mirror

"As he [the sinner] beholds the righteousness of Christ in the divine precepts, he exclaims, 'The law of the Lord is perfect, converting the soul.' As the sinner is pardoned for his transgression through the merits of Christ, as he is clothed with the righteousness of Christ through faith in Him, he declares with the psalmist, 'How sweet are Thy words unto my taste! Yea, sweeter than honey to my mouth.' 'More to be desired are they than gold, yea, than much fine gold; sweeter also than honey and the honeycomb.' This is conversion."–*Review and Herald, June 21, 1892.*

The Law Demands Righteousness

"The law demands righteousness, and this the sinner owes to the law; but he is incapable of rendering it."–*Review and Herald, Nov. 4, 1890.*

"Notwithstanding all the profession of lip and voice, if the character is not in harmony with the law of God, those making profession of godliness bear evil fruit."–*Review and Herald, May 5, 1901.*

The Only Provision for Meeting the Demands of the Law

"Man cannot possibly meet the demands of the law of God in human strength alone. His offerings, his works, will all be tainted with sin.

A remedy has been provided in the Saviour, who can give to man the virtue of His merit, and make him co-laborer in the great rock of salvation. Christ is righteousness, sanctification, and redemption to those who believe in Him, and who follow in His steps." –*Review and Herald, Feb. 4, 1890.*

"By His perfect obedience He has made it possible for every human being to obey God's commandments. When we submit ourselves to Christ, the heart is united with His heart, the will is merged in His will, the mind becomes one with His mind, the thoughts are brought into captivity to Him; we live His life. This is what it means to be clothed with the garments of His righteousness. Then as the Lord looks upon us, He sees, not the fig-leaf garment, not the nakedness and deformity of sin, but His own robe of righteousness, which is perfect obedience to the law of Jehovah."– *"Christ's Object Lessons," page 312.*

"The only way in which he [the sinner] can attain to righteousness is through faith. By faith he can bring to God the merits of Christ, and the Lord places the obedience of His Son to the sinner's account. Christ's righteousness is accepted in place of man's failure, and God receives, pardons, justifies, the repentant, believing soul, treats him as though he were righteous, and loves him as He loves His Son. This is how faith is accounted righteousness; and the pardoned soul goes on from grace to grace, from light to a greater light. He can say with rejoicing, 'Not by works of righteousness which we have done, but according to His mercy He saved us, by the washing of regeneration, and renewing or the Holy Ghost; which He shed on us abundantly through Jesus Christ our Saviour, that being justified by His grace, we should be made heirs according to the hope of eternal life.'" –*Review and Herald, Nov. 4, 1890.*

"Christ gave His life as a sacrifice, not to destroy God's law, not to create a lower standard, but to maintain justice, and to give man a second probation. No one can keep God's commandments except in

Christ's power. He bore in His body the sins of all mankind, and He imputes His righteousness to every believing child."–*Review and Herald, May 7, 1901.*

"The law has no power to pardon the transgressor, but it points him to Christ Jesus, who says to him, I will take your sin and bear it Myself, if you will accept Me as your substitute and surety. Return to your allegiance, and I will impute to you My righteousness."–*Review and Herald, May 7, 1901.*

"The death of Christ was an argument in man's behalf that could not be overthrown. The penalty of the law fell upon him who was equal with God, and man was free to accept the righteousness of Christ, and by a life of penitence and humiliation to triumph, as the Son of God had triumphed, over the power of Satan. Thus God is just, and yet the justifier of all who believe in Jesus."–*"The Great Controversy," pp. 502, 503.*

The Divine Plan in Presenting the Claims of the Law

"If we would have the spirit and power of the third angel's message, we must present the law and the gospel together, for they go hand in hand."–*Review and Herald, Sept. 3, 1889.*

"Many sermons preached upon the claims of the law have been without Christ, and this lack has made the truth inefficient in converting souls."–*Review and Herald, Feb. 3, 1891.*

"In presenting the binding claims of the law, many have failed to portray the infinite love of Christ. Those who have so great truths, so weighty reforms, to present to the people, have not had a realization of the value of the atoning Sacrifice as an expression of God's great love to man. Love for Jesus, and Jesus' love for sinners, have been dropped out of the religious experience of those who have been commissioned to preach the gospel, and self has been exalted instead of the Redeemer of mankind."–*Review and Herald*, Feb. 3, 1891.

THE REMNANT CHURCH IN GRAVE DANGER

Conditions Pointed Out

Spiritual Paralysis

"All through our churches there are those who are spiritually paralyzed. They do not manifest spiritual life."—*Review and Herald, May 24, 1892.*

Spiritual Lethargy

"The slumbering church must be aroused, awakened out of its spiritual lethargy, to a realization of the important duties which have been left undone. The people have not entered into the holy place, where Jesus has gone to make an atonement for His children."—*Review and Herald, Feb. 25, 1890.*

Spiritual Slumber

"That which Satan has led men to do in the past, he will, if possible, lead them to do again. The early church was deceived by the enemy of God and man, and apostasy was brought into the ranks of those who professed to love God; and today, unless the people of God awake out of sleep, they will be taken unawares by the devices of Satan. Among those who claim to believe in the near coming of the Saviour, how many are backslidden, how many have lost their first love, and come under the description of the Laodicean church, denominating them as neither cold nor hot. Satan will do his utmost to keep them in a state of indifference and stupor. May the Lord reveal to the people the perils that are before them, that they may arouse from their spiritual slumber, and trim their lamps, and be found watching for the Bridegroom when He shall return from the wedding." –*Review and Herald, Nov. 22, 1892.*

Spiritual Blindness

"There are many, many professed Christians who are waiting unconcernedly for the coming of the Lord. They have not on the garment of His righteousness. They may profess to be children of God, but they are not cleansed from sin. They are selfish and self-sufficient. Their experience is Christless. They neither love God supremely nor their neighbor as themselves. They have no true idea of what constitutes holiness. They do not see the defects in themselves. So blinded are they, that they are not able to detect the subtle working of pride and iniquity. They are clad in the rags of self-righteousness, and stricken with spiritual blindness. Satan has cast his shadow between them and Christ, and they have no wish to study the pure, holy character of the Saviour."– *Review and Herald, Feb. 26, 1901.*

Spiritual Drought

"We need the Holy Spirit in order to understand the truths for this time; but there is spiritual drought in the churches, and we have accustomed ourselves to be easily satisfied with our standing before God."– *Review and Herald, Feb. 25, 1890.*

Churches Dying

"Our churches are dying for the want of teaching on the subject of righteousness by faith in Christ, and on kindred truths."–*"Gospel Workers," p. 301.*

Danger of Making a Terrible Mistake

"If we are self-sufficient, and think that we may go on just as we please, and yet hope to come out on the right side finally, we shall find that we have made a terrible mistake." –*Review and Herald,* July 9, 1908.

Partial Work not Sufficient

"We must be emptied of self. But this is not all that is required; for when we have renounced our idols, the vacuum must be supplied. If the heart is left desolate, and the vacuum not supplied, it will be swept, and garnished,' but without a guest to occupy it. The evil spirit took unto himself seven other spirits more wicked than himself, and they entered in and dwelt there; and the last state of that man was worse than the first.

"As you empty the heart of self, you must accept the righteousness of Christ. Lay hold of it by faith; for you must have the mind and spirit of Christ that you may work the works of Christ. If you open the door of the heart, Jesus will supply the vacuum by the gift of His Spirit, and then you can be a living preacher in your home, in the church, and in the world." –*Review and Herald, Feb. 23, 1892.*

"It is not enough to make the heart empty; we must have the vacuum filled with the love of God. The soul must be furnished with the graces of the Spirit of God. We may leave off many bad habits, and yet not be truly sanctified, because we do not have a connection with God."–*Review and Herald, Jan. 24, 1893.*

THE GREAT NEED OF THE CHURCH

"A revival of true godliness among us is the greatest and most urgent of all our needs. To seek this should be our first work. There must be earnest effort to obtain the blessing of the Lord, not because God is not willing to bestow His blessing upon us, but because we are unprepared to receive it. Our heavenly Father is more willing to give His Holy Spirit to them that ask Him, than are earthly parents to give good gifts to their children. But it is our work, by confession, humiliation, repentance, and earnest prayer, to fulfil the conditions upon which God has promised to grant us His blessing.

"A revival need be expected only in answer to prayer. While the people are so destitute of God's Holy Spirit; they cannot appreciate the preaching of the word; but when the Spirit's power touches their hearts, then the discourses given will not be without effect. Guided by the teachings of God's Word with the manifestation of His Spirit, in the exercise of sound discretion, those who attend our meetings will gain a precious experience, and returning home will be prepared to exert a healthful influence.

"The old standard-bearers knew what it was to wrestle with God in prayer, and to enjoy the outpouring of His Spirit. But these are passing off from the stage of action; and who are coming up to fill their places? How is it with the rising generation? Are they converted to God? Are we awake to the work that is going on in the heavenly sanctuary, or are we waiting for some compelling power to come upon the church before we shall arouse? Are we hoping to see the whole church revived? That time will never come.

"There are persons in the church who are not converted, and who will not unite in earnest, prevailing prayer. We must enter upon the work individually. We must pray more, and talk less. Iniquity abounds, and the people must be taught not to be satisfied with a form of godliness without the spirit and power. If we are intent upon searching our own hearts, putting away our sins, and correcting our evil tendencies, our souls will not be lifted up unto vanity; we shall be distrustful of our-

113

selves, having an abiding sense that our sufficiency is of God.

"We have far more to fear from within than from without. The hindrances to strength and success are far greater from the church itself than from the world. Unbelievers have a right to expect that those who profess to be keeping the commandments of God and the faith of Jesus, will do more than any other class to promote and honor, by their consistent lives, by their godly example and their active influence, the cause which they represent. But how often have the professed advocates of the truth proved the greatest obstacle to its advancement! The unbelief indulged, the doubts expressed, the darkness cherished, encourage the presence of evil angels, and open the way for the accomplishment of Satan's devices.

"The adversary of souls is not permitted to read the thoughts of men; but he is a keen observer, and he marks the words; he takes account of actions, and skilfully adapts his temptations to meet the cases of those who place themselves in his power. If we would labor to repress sinful thoughts and feelings, giving them no expression in words or actions, Satan would be defeated; for he could not prepare his specious temptations to meet the case. But how often do professed Christians, by their lack of self-control, open the door to the adversary of souls! Divisions, and even bitter dissensions which would disgrace any worldly community, are common in the churches, because there is so little effort to control wrong feelings, and to repress every word that Satan can take advantage of. As soon as an alienation of feeling arises, the matter is spread before Satan for his inspection, and the opportunity given for him to use his serpent-like wisdom and skill in dividing and destroying the church.

"There is great loss in every dissension. Personal friends of both parties take sides with their respective favorites, and thus the breach is widened. A house divided against itself cannot stand. Criminations and recriminations are engendered and multiplied. Satan and his angels are actively at work to secure a harvest from seed thus sown. Worldlings look on, and jeeringly exclaim, 'Behold how these Christians hate one another! If this is religion, we do not want it.' And they look upon themselves and their irreligious characters with great satisfaction. Thus they are confirmed in their impenitence, and Satan exults at his success.

"The great deceiver has prepared his wiles for every soul that is not braced for trial and guarded by constant prayer and living faith. As ministers, as Christians, we must work to take the stumbling blocks out of the way. We must remove every obstacle. Let us confess and forsake every sin, that the way of the Lord may be prepared, that He may come into our assemblies and impart His rich grace. The world, the flesh, and the devil must be overcome. We cannot prepare the way by gaining the friendship of the world, which is enmity with God; but by His help we can break its seductive influence upon ourselves and upon others. We cannot individually or as a body secure ourselves from the constant temptations of a relentless and determined foe; but in the strength of Jesus we can resist them. From every member of the church a steady light may shine forth before the world, so that they shall not be led to inquire, What do these people more than others? There can be and must be a withdrawal from conformity to the world, a shunning of all appearance of evil, so that no occasion shall be given for gainsayers. We cannot escape reproach; it will come; but we should be very careful that we are not reproached for our own sins or follies, but for Christ's sake.

"There is nothing that Satan fears so much as that the people of God shall clear the way by removing every hindrance, so that the Lord can pour out His Spirit upon a languishing church and an impenitent congregation. If Satan had his way, there would never be another awakening, great or small, to the end of time. But we are not ignorant of his devices. It is possible to resist his power. When the way is prepared for the spirit of God, the blessing will come. Satan can no more hinder a shower of blessing from descending upon God's people than he can close the windows of heaven that rain cannot come upon the earth. Wicked men and devils cannot hinder the work of God, or shut out His presence from the assemblies of His people, if they will, with subdued, contrite hearts, confess and put away their sins, and in faith claim His promises. Every temptation, every opposing influence, whether open or secret, may be successfully resisted, 'not by might, nor by power, but by My Spirit, saith the Lord of hosts.'

"We are in the great day of atonement, when our sins are, by confession and repentance, to go beforehand to judgment. God does not now accept a tame, spiritless testimony from His ministers. Such a testimony would not be present truth. The message for this time must be meat in due season to feed the church of God. But Satan has been seeking gradually to rob this message of its power, that the people may not be prepared to stand in the day of the Lord.

"In 1844 our great High Priest entered the most holy place of the heavenly sanctuary, to begin the work of the investigative judgment. The cases of the righteous dead have been passing in review before God. When that work shall be completed, judgment is to be pronounced upon the living. How precious how important, are these solemn moments! Each of us has a case pending in the court of heaven. We are individually to be judged according to the deeds done in the body. In the typical service, when the work of atonement was performed by the high priest in the most holy place of the earthly sanctuary, the people were required to afflict their souls before God, and confess their sins. That they might be atoned for and blotted out. Will any less be required of us in this antitypical day of atonement, when Christ in the sanctuary above is pleading in behalf of His people, and the final irrevocable decision is to be pronounced upon every case?

"What is our condition in this fearful and solemn time? Alas, what pride is prevailing in the church, what hypocrisy, what deception, what love of dress, frivolity, and amusement, what desire for the supremacy! All these sins have clouded the mind, so that eternal things have not been discerned. Shall we not search the Scriptures, that we may know where we are in this world's history? Shall we not become intelligent in regard to the work that is being accomplished for us at this time, and the position that we as sinners should occupy while this work of atonement is going forward? If we have any regard for our souls' salvation, we must make a decided change. We must seek the Lord with true penitence; we must with deep contrition of soul confess our sins, that they may be blotted out.

"We must no longer remain upon the enchanted ground. We are fast approaching the close of our probation. Let every soul inquire, How do I stand before God? We know not how soon our names may be taken into the lips of Christ, and our cases be finally decided. What, oh, what will these decisions be? Shall we be counted with the righteous, or shall we be numbered with the wicked?

"Let the church arise, and repent of her backslidings before God. Let the watchmen awake, and give the trumpet a certain sound. It is a definite warning that we have to proclaim. God commands His servants, 'Cry aloud, spare not, lift up thy voice like a trumpet, and show My people their transgression, and the house of Jacob their sins.' The attention of the people must be gained; unless this can be done all effort is useless; though an angel from heaven should come down and speak to them, his words would do no more good than if he were speaking into the cold ear of death. The church must arouse to action. The Spirit of God can never come in until she prepares the way. There should be earnest searching of heart. There should be united, persevering prayer, and through faith a claiming of the promises of God. There should be, not a clothing of the body with sackcloth, as in ancient times, but a deep humiliation of soul. We have not the first reason for self-congratulation and self-exaltation. We should humble ourselves under the mighty hand of God, He will appear to comfort and bless the true seekers.

"The work is before us; will we engage in it? We must work fast, we must go steadily forward. We must be preparing for the great day of the Lord. We have no time to lose, no time to be engaged in selfish purposes. The world is to be warned. What are we doing as individuals to bring the light before others? God has left to every man his work; everyone has a part to act, and we cannot neglect this work except at the peril of our souls.

"O my brethren, will you grieve the Holy Spirit, and cause it to depart? Will you shut out the blessed Saviour, because you are unprepared for His presence? Will you leave souls to perish without the knowledge of the truth, because you love your ease too well to bear the burden that Jesus bore for you? Let us awake out of sleep. 'Be sober, be vigilant; because your adversary the devil, as a roaring lion, walketh about, seeking whom he may devour.'" –*Review and Herald, March 22, 1887*.

THE CALL FOR A SPIRITUAL REVIVAL AND REFORMATION

"'Nevertheless I have somewhat against thee, because thou hast left thy first love. Remember therefore from whence thou art fallen, and repent, and do the first works; or else I will come unto thee quickly, and will remove thy candlestick out of his place, except thou repent.'

"I am instructed to say that these words are applicable to Seventh-day Adventist churches in their present condition. The love of God has been lost, and this means the absence of love for one another. Self, self,

118

self is cherished, and is striving for the supremacy. How long is this to continue? Unless there is a reconversion, there will soon be such a lack of godliness, that the church will be represented by the barren fig tree. Great light has been given to her. She has had abundant opportunity for bearing much fruit. But selfishness has come in, and God says, 'I.... will remove thy candlestick out of his place, except thou repent.'

"Jesus looked upon the pretentious, fruitless fig tree, and with mournful reluctance pronounced the words of doom. And under the curse of an offended God, the fig tree withered away. God help His people to make an application of this lesson while there is still time.

"Just before His ascension, Christ said to His disciples, 'All power is given unto Me in heaven and in earth. Go ye therefore, and teach all nations, baptizing them in the name of the Father, and of the Son, and of the Holy Ghost; teaching them to observe all things whatsoever I have commanded you: and, lo, I am with you always, even unto the end of the world.' God's people today are not fulfilling this commission as they should. Selfishness prevents them from receiving these words in their solemn significance.

"In many hearts there seems to be scarcely a breath of spiritual life. This makes me very sad. I fear that aggressive warfare against the world, the flesh, and the devil has not been maintained. Shall we cheer on, by a half-dead Christianity, the selfish, covetous spirit of the world, sharing its ungodliness and smiling on its falsehood? Nay! By the grace of God let us be steadfast to the principles of truth, holding firm to the end the beginning of our confidence. We are to be 'not slothful in business; fervent in spirit; serving the Lord.' One is our Master, even Christ. To Him we are to look. From Him we are to receive our wisdom. By His grace we are to preserve our integrity, standing before God in meekness and contrition, and representing Him to the world.

"Sermons have been in great demand in our churches. The members have depended upon pulpit declamations instead of on the Holy Spirit. Uncalled for and unused, the spiritual gifts bestowed on them have dwindled into feebleness. If the ministers would go forth into new fields, the members would be obliged to bear responsibilities, and by use their capabilities would increase.

"God brings against ministers and people the heavy charge of spiritual feebleness, saying, 'I know thy works, that thou art neither cold nor hot: I would thou wert cold or hot. So then because thou art lukewarm, and neither cold nor hot, I will spew thee out of My mouth. Because thou sayest, I am rich, and increased with goods, and have need of nothing; and knowest not that thou art wretched, and miserable, and poor, and blind, and naked: I counsel thee to buy of Me gold tried in the fire, that thou mayest be rich; and white raiment, that thou mayest be clothed, and that the shame of thy nakedness do not appear; and anoint thine eyes with eyesalve, that thou mayest see.'

"God calls for a spiritual revival and a spiritual reformation. Unless this takes place, those who are lukewarm will continue to grow more abhorrent to the Lord, until He will refuse to acknowledge them as His children.

"A revival and a reformation must take place under the ministration of the Holy Spirit. Revival and reformation are two different things. Revival signifies a renewal of spiritual life, a quickening of the powers of mind and heart, a resurrection from spiritual death. Reformation signifies a reorganization, a change in ideas and theories, habits and practices. Reformation will not bring forth the good fruit of righteousness unless it is connected with the revival of the Spirit. Revival and reformation are to do their appointed work and in doing this work they must be blend.

"'Ye are not your own; for ye are bought with a price: therefore glorify God in your body, and in your spirit, which are God's' 'Let your light so shine before men, that they may see your good works, and glorify your Father which is in heaven.' Christ gave His life for a fallen race, leaving us an example that we should follow in His steps. To him who does this will be spoken the words of approval, 'Well done, good and faithful servant; . . . enter thou into the joy of thy Lord.'

"The word of the Lord never represses activity. It increases man's usefulness by guiding his activities in the right direction. The Lord does not leave man without an object of pursuit. He places before him an immortal inheritance, and gives him ennobling truth, that he may advance in a safe and sure path, in pursuit of that which is worth the consecration of his highest capabilities, –a crown of everlasting life.

"Man will increase in power as he follows on to know the Lord. As he endeavors to reach the highest standard, the Bible is as a light to guide his footsteps homeward. In that word he finds that he is a joint heir with Christ to an eternal treasure. The Guidebook points him to the unsearchable riches of heaven. By following on to know the Lord, he is securing never-ending happiness. Day by day the peace of God is his reward, and by faith he sees a home of everlasting sunshine, free from all sorrow and disappointment. God directs his footsteps, and keeps him from falling.

"God loves His church. There are tares mingled with the wheat, but the Lord knows His own. 'Thou has a few names even in Sardis which have not defiled their garments; and they shall walk with me in white: for they are worthy. He that overcometh, the same shall be clothed in white raiment; and I will not blot out his name out of the book of life, but I will confess his name before My Father, and before His angels. He that hath an ear, let him hear what the Spirit saith unto the churches.'

"Shall not the counsel of Christ have an effect on the churches? Why halt, ye who know the truth, between two opinions? 'If the Lord be God, follow Him: but if Baal, then follow him.' Christ's followers have no right to stand on the ground of neutrality. There is more hope of an open enemy than of one who is neutral.

"Let the church respond to the words of the prophet, 'Arise, shine; for thy light is come, and the glory of the Lord is risen upon thee. For, behold, the darkness shall cover the earth, and gross darkness the people: but the Lord shall arise upon thee, and His glory shall be seen upon thee.'

"God's people have lost their first love. They must now repent and make steady advancement in the path of holiness. God's purposes reach to every phase of life. They are immutable, eternal; and at the time appointed they will be executed. For a time it may seem that Satan has all the power in his hands; but our trust is in God. When we draw near to Him, He will draw near to us, and will work with mighty power to accomplish His gracious purposes.

"God rebukes His people for their sins, that He may humble them, and lead them to seek His face. As they reform, and His love revives in their hearts, His loving answers will come to their requests. He will strengthen them in reformatory action, lifting up for them a standard against the enemy. His rich blessing will rest upon them, and in bright rays they will reflect the light of heaven. Then a multitude not of their faith, seeing that God is with His people, will unite with them in serving the Redeemer."–*Review and Herald, Feb. 25, 1902.*

A Reformatory Movement

"God calls upon those who are willing to be controlled by the Holy Spirit to lead out in a work of thorough reformation. I see a crisis before us, and the Lord calls for His laborers to come into line. Every soul should now stand in a position of deeper, truer consecration to God than during the years that have passed. . . I have been deeply impressed by scenes that have recently passed before me in the night season. There seemed to be a great movement–a work of revival–going forward in many places. Our people were moving into line, responding to God's call. My brethren, the Lord is speaking to us. Shall we not heed His voice? Shall we not trim our lamps and act like men who look for their Lord to come? The time is one that calls for light-bearing, for action."– *"Testimonies to Ministers and Gospel Workers," pp. 514, 515.*

"The time has come for a thorough reformation to take place. When this reformation begins, the spirit of prayer will actuate every believer, and will banish from the church the spirit of discord and strife. Those who have not been living in Christian fellowship will draw close to one another. One member working in right lines will lead other members to unite with him in making intercession for the revelation of the Holy Spirit. There will be no confusion, because all will be in harmony with the mind of the spirit. The barriers separating believer from believer will be broken down, and God's servants will speak the same things. The Lord will cooperate with His servants. All will pray understandingly the prayer that Christ taught His servants: 'Thy kingdom come. Thy will be done in earth, as it is in heaven.' Matt. 6:10."– *"Testimonies for the Church," Vol. VIII, page 251.*

"In visions of the night representations passed before me of a great reformatory movement among God's people. Many were praising God. The sick were healed, and other miracles were wrought. A spirit of intercession was seen, even as was manifested before the great day of Pentecost. Hundreds and thousands were seen visiting families, and opening before them the Word of God. Hearts were convicted by the power of the Holy Spirit, and a spirit of genuine conversion was manifest. On every side doors were thrown open to the proclamation of the truth. The world seemed to be lightened with the heavenly influence. Great blessings were received by the true and humble people of God. I heard voices of thanksgiving and praise, and there seemed to be a reformation such as we witnessed in 1844."– *"Testimonies for the Church," Vol. IX, p. 126.*

THE PERILS AND PRIVILEGES OF THE LAST DAYS

"To the early church the hope of Christ's coming was a blessed hope, and they were represented by the apostle as waiting for His Son from heaven as loving His appearing. As long as this hope was cherished by the professed followers of Christ, they were a light to the world. But it was not the design of Satan that they should be a light to the world. . . Satan was at work to cause apostasy in the early church; and in accomplishing his purpose, doctrines were introduced through which the church was leavened with unbelief in Christ and His coming. The adversary of God and man cast his hellish shadow athwart the path of the believers and dimmed their star of hope, even their faith in the glorious appearing of the great God and our Saviour Jesus Christ.

"The hope which had been so precious to them lost its attractions; for the specious delusions of Satan almost wholly extinguished the light of salvation through the merits of a crucified and risen Saviour, and men were led to seek to make an atonement through works of their own, –by fasts and penances, and through the payment of money to the church. It was more agreeable to the natural heart thus to seek justification than to seek it through repentance and faith, through belief in, and obedience to, the truth.

"During the ages of apostasy, darkness covered the earth, and gross darkness the people; but the Reformation aroused the inhabitants of earth from their deathlike slumber, and many turned away from their vanities and superstitions, from priests and penances, to serve the living God, to search in His Holy Word for truth as for hidden treasure. They began diligently to work the mine of truth, to clear away the rubbish of

124

human opinion that had buried up the precious jewels of light. But as soon as the work of reformation began, Satan with determined purpose sought the more zealously to bind the minds of men in superstition and error. . . .

"That which Satan has led men to do in the past, he will if possible lead them to do again. The early church was deceived by the enemy of God and man, and apostasy was brought into the ranks of those who professed to love God; and today, unless the people of God awake out of sleep, they will be taken unawares by the devices of Satan. Among those who claim to believe in the near coming of the Saviour, how many are backslidden, how many have lost their first love, and come under the description written of the Laodicean church, denominating them as neither cold not hot. Satan will do his utmost to keep them in a state of indifference and stupor. May the Lord reveal to the people the perils that are before them, that they may arouse from their spiritual slumber, and trim their lamps and be found watching for the Bridegroom when He shall return from the wedding.

"The days in which we live are eventful and full of peril. The signs of the coming of the end are thickening around us, and events are to come to pass that will be of a more terrible character than any the world has yet witnessed. . .

"Let everyone who claims to believe that the Lord is soon coming, search the Scriptures as never before; for Satan is determined to try every device possible to keep souls in darkness, and blind the mind to the perils of the times in which we are living. Let every believer take up his Bible with earnest prayer, that he may be enlightened by the Holy Spirit as to what is truth, that he may know more of God and of Jesus Christ whom He has sent. Search for the truth as for hidden treasures, and disappoint the enemy.

"The time of test is just upon us, for the loud cry of the third angel has already begun in the revelation of the righteousness of Christ, the sin-pardoning Redeemer. This is the beginning of the light of the angel whose glory shall fill the whole earth.

"It is the work of everyone to whom the message of warning has come, to lift up Jesus, to present Him to the world as revealed in types, as shadowed in symbols, as manifested in the revelations of the prophets, as unveiled in the lessons given to His disciples and in the wonderful miracles wrought for the sons of men. Search the Scriptures; for they are they that testify of Him.

"If you would stand through the time of trouble, you must know Christ, and appropriate the gift of His righteousness, which He imputes to the repentant sinner. Human wisdom will not avail to devise a plan of salvation. Human philosophy is vain, the fruits of the loftiest powers of man are worthless, aside from the great plan of the divine Teacher. No glory is to redound to man; all human help and glory lies in the dust; for the truth as it is in Jesus is the only available agent by which man may be saved. Man is privileged to connect with Christ, and then the divine and the human combine; and in this union the hope of man must rest alone; for it is as the Spirit of God touches the soul that the powers of the soul are quickened, and man becomes a new creature in Christ Jesus. . . .

"The theme that attracts the heart of the sinner is Christ and Him crucified. On the cross of Calvary, Jesus stands revealed to the world in unparalleled love. Present Him thus to the hungering multitudes, and the light of His love will win men from darkness to light, from transgression to obedience and true holiness. Beholding Jesus upon the cross of Calvary arouses the conscience to the heinous character of sin as nothing else can do. It was sin that caused the death of God's dear Son, and sin is the transgression of the law. On Him was laid the iniquity of us all. The sinner then consents unto the law that it is good; for he realizes that it condemns his evil deeds, while it magnifies the matchless love of God in providing for him salvation through the imputed right-eousness of Him who knew no sin, in whose mouth there was found no guile.

"The truth is efficient, and through obedience its power changes the mind into the image of Jesus. It is the truth as it is in Jesus that quick-ens the conscience and transforms the mind; for it is accompanied to the heart by the Holy Spirit. There are many who, lacking spiritual dis-cernment, take the bare letter of the word, and find that unaccompa-nied by the Spirit of God, it quickens not the soul, it sanctifies not the heart. One may be able to quote from the Old and the New Testament, may be familiar with the commands and promises of the Word of God; but unless the Holy Spirit sends the truth home to the heart, enlighten-ing the mind with divine light, no soul falls upon the Rock and is bro-ken; for it is the divine agency that connects the soul with God. With-out the enlightenment of the Spirit of God, we shall not be able to dis-cern truth from error, and shall fall under the masterful temptations and deceptions that Satan will bring upon the world.

"We are near the close of the controversy between the prince of light and the prince of darkness, and soon the delusions of the enemy will try our faith, of what sort it is. Satan will work miracles in the sight of the beast, and deceive 'them that dwell on the earth by the means of those miracles which he had power to do in the sight of the beast.' But though the prince of darkness will work to cover the earth with dark-ness, and with gross darkness the people, the Lord will manifest His converting power. . . .

"The work of the Holy Spirit is immeasurably great. It is from this source that power and efficiency come to the worker for God; and the Holy Spirit is the Comforter, and the personal presence of Christ to the soul. He who looks to Christ in simple, childlike faith, is made a partak-er of the divine nature through the agency of the Holy Spirit. When led by the Spirit of God, the Christian may know that he is made complete in Him who is the head of all things. As Christ was glorified on the day of Pentecost, so will He again be glorified in the closing work of the gospel, when He shall prepare a people to stand the final test in the closing conflict of the great controversy. . . .

"When the earth is lightened with the glory of God, we shall see a work similar to that which was wrought when the disciples, filled with the Holy Spirit, proclaimed the power of a risen Saviour. The light of heaven penetrated the darkened minds of those who had been deceived by the enemies of Christ, and the false representation of Him was rejected; for through the efficiency of the Holy Spirit they now saw Him exalted to be a prince and Saviour, to give repentance unto Israel, and remission of sins. They saw Him encircled with the glory of heaven, with infinite treasures in His hands to bestow upon those who turn from their rebellion. As the apostles set forth the glory of the only begotten of the Father, three thousand souls were pricked to the heart, and they were made to see themselves as they were, sinful and polluted, and Christ as their Saviour and Redeemer,. Christ was lifted up, Christ was glorified, through the power of the Holy Spirit resting upon men. By the eye of faith these believers saw Him as the one who had borne humiliation, suffering, and death, that they might not perish, but have everlasting life. As they looked upon His spotless righteousness, they saw their own deformity and pollution, and were filled with godly fear, with love and adoration for Him who gave His life a sacrifice for them. They humbled their souls to the very dust, and repented of their wicked works, and glorified God for His salvation. . . .

"The revelation of Christ by the Holy Spirit brought to them a realizing sense of His power and majesty, and they stretched forth their hands unto Him by faith, saying, 'I believe.' Thus it was in the time of the early rain; but the latter rain will be more abundant. The Saviour of men will be glorified, and the earth will be lightened with the bright shining of the beams of His righteousness. He is the fountain of light, and light from the gates ajar has been shining upon the people of God that they may lift Him up in His glorious character before those who sit in darkness.

"Christ has not been presented in connection with the law as a faithful and merciful High Priest, who was in all points tempted like as we are, yet without sin. He has not been lifted up before the sinner as the divine sacrifice. His work as sacrifice, substitute, and surety, has been only coldly and casually dwelt upon; but this is what the sinner needs to know. It is Christ in His fullness as a sin-pardoning Saviour, that the sinner must see; for the unparalleled love of Christ, through the agency of the Holy Spirit, will bring conviction and conversion to the hardened heart.

"It is the divine influence that is the savor of the salt in the Christian. Many present the doctrines and theories of our faith; but their presentation is as salt without savor; for the Holy Spirit is not working through their faithless ministry. They have not opened the heart to receive the grace of Christ; they know not the operation of the Spirit; they are as meal without leaven; for there is no working principle in all their labor, and they fail to win souls to Christ. They do not appropriate the righteousness of Christ; it is a robe unworn by them, a fullness unknown, a fountain untouched.

"O that the atoning work of Christ might be carefully studied! O that all would carefully and prayerfully study the Word of God, not to qualify themselves for debating controverted points of doctrine, but that as hungry souls they might be filled, as those that thirst, be refreshed at the fountain of life. It is when we search the Scriptures with humble hearts, feeling our weakness and unworthiness, that Jesus is revealed to our souls in all His preciousness.

"When we become partakers of the divine nature, we shall look with abhorrence upon all our exaltation of self, and that which we have cherished as wisdom, will seem as dross and rubbish. Those who have educated themselves as debaters, who have looked upon themselves as sharp keen men, will view their work with sorrow and shame, and know that their offering has been as valueless as was Cain's; for it has been destitute of the righteousness of Christ.

"O that we as a people might humble our hearts before God, and plead with Him for the endowment of the Holy Spirit! If we came to the Lord in humility and contrition of soul, He would answer our petitions; for He says that he is more willing to give us the Holy Spirit than are parents to give good gifts to their children. Then would Christ be glorified, and in Him we should discern the fullness of the godhead bodily. For Christ has said of the Comforter, 'He shall glorify Me; for He shall receive of Mine, and shall show it unto you.' This is the thing most essential to us. For 'this is life eternal, that they might know thee, the only true God, and Jesus Christ whom Thou hast sent.'"–*Review and Herald, Nov. 22 and 29, 1892.*

TEXTUAL INDEX

Page

Gen. 6:9 17

Gen. 7:1 17

Psalms 11:7 .... 14, 16

Psalms 36:6 16

Psalms 92:15. .... 14, 16

Psalms 119:142 16

Psalms 145:17 16

Dn. 9:7 16

Matt. 23:35 17

Luke 1:6 17

John 5:17 16

Rom. 1:16, 17 .... 18, 61

Rom. 1:29 17

Rom. 3 19

Rom. 3:10 17

Rom. 3:20-22 19

Rom. 3:21, 22 21

Rom. 3:22-25 19

Rom. 3:23 17

Rom. 3:24, 25 22

Rom. 4:1 19

Rom. 4:2 20

Rom. 4:3 17,20

Rom. 4:5 20

Rom. 4:6 20

Rom. 4:9 20

Rom. 4:21-25 21

Page

Rom. 5:1 ....23, 60

Rom. 5:1-5 62

Rom. 6:17-22 18

Rom. 7:14... 17

Rom. 7:18 17

Rom. 9:30 ....18, 23

Rom. 9:31, 32 23

Rom. 10:3, 4 23

Rom. 10:8-10 24

1 Cor. 15:34 ....14, 16

Eph. 4:22-24 16

Eph. 5:9 16

1 Tim. 6:11 16

Heb. 1:9 16

Heb. 11:4 17

2 Peter 2:7, 8 17

2 Peter 2:7, 8 18

Rev. 3:18... 2

Rev. 14:6 60

Rev. 14:7 60

Rev. 14:12 60

Rev. 18:1, 2 54

TOPICAL INDEX

	Page
1844	116,123
1887 - messages of	8,32,33,35,36,74,78,118
1888	3,9,27,29,30,32,36-38,40,42,50,53-55,58,63,79
1889	44-47,51,52,69,70,74,77,79,80,82,93,109
1890	22,44,45,47-50,59,61,73,74,78,83-86,89,90,
	92-96,101-103,106-108,110,111
1891	54,109,110
1892	53,57,58,67,70,73,74,76,83,84,88,90,97,104,
	105,107,110,112,130
1893	73,78,85,88,112
1894	76-78,81,83,103
1895	70,76,83,87,89
1896	68
1899	70,73,76,96,97
1900	68
1901	107,109,111
1902	92,122
1903	84
1904	75,79,91
1905	68
1907	100
1908	75,77,91,112
1911	68
1924	8
1926	6
A	
Abel	17
Abraham	17,19,20,74
Account - sinner's	19,22,108
Adam	15,17,18,82,86
Advent - second	42
Adversary of God	124
Adversary of souls	114

TOPICAL INDEX (Cont'd)

A (Cont'd) **Page**

Adversary the devil 118
Anchorage - safe 38
Anoint 16,52,102,103,120
Approval - seal of 27
Atonement, day of 116

B

Baal 121
Belief - in God 20
Belief - in truth 73,124
Belief - intellectual 73
Bible 8,31,32,72,76,79,121,125
Blindness - spiritual 50,51,111
Body 109,115-117,120

C

Cain 130
Calvary 19,37,51,52,56,72,84,85,87,126
Character 24,31,37,43,47,48,53,56,60,73,75-77,84,
...... 88,90,94,95,100, 101,103,106,107,111,115,125,126,129
Character - Christian 32,75,76
Character - God 24,37,47,75,77,88,90,103,111,129
Character - immutable 37
Character - sin 56,84,101,115,125,126
Christ - atoning blood of 36
Christ - blood of 19,36,52
Christ - comforter 15
Christ - coronation of 91
Christ - deliverer 15,97
Christ - fellowship with 32,62,92,95,94
Christ - life-giver 15
Christ - mediatorial work of 106
Christ - our righteousness 15
Christ - power of 15,95,101
Christ - union with 35,36

TOPICAL INDEX (Cont'd)

C (Cont'd)   **Page**
Christ - vine - living 35
Church 8,10,11,27,29,30-38,41,42,44-46,50-52
.... 55,68,72,75,76,78,80,82-84,90,106,110,
.... 111-119,121-125
Church - languishing 34,115
Church - Laodicean 45,110,125
Church - remnant 8,10,31,42,55,110
Comforter 15,57,127,130
Commission - Great 37,52,109,119
Compassion 20,22,46,94,105
Conflict 11,17,22,42,49,62,128
Confused people 49
Consecration 38,121,122
Contemplating 77
Controversy, Great 109,128
Conviction 9,27,37,43,53,57,60,75,129
Creation 15,72
Crisis 122
Criticize 48-50
Cross 19,37,39,44,56,68,69,72,75,84-87,101,126
Crown 11,91,121
Crucifixion of self 46
Cry - loud 53-58,125
D
Daniells, A.G. 5,8
Deeds 17,18,22,86,87,116,126
Deliverance 19,21,69,94
Des Moines 8
Divine nature 9,86,87,88,127,129
Dogma 36
Drifting - members 32,34,38
Duty 43,77,83,96
E
Ebb - low 75

TOPICAL INDEX (Cont'd)

E (Cont'd)   **Page**
Elisabeth 17
Era - new 27,53
Estrangement 43
Excitement - undue 45
Exhortation 48
Experience - living 62,80,81
Explanation 10,54
Ezra 35
F
Failure - Israel's 23
Failure - man's 22,108
Faith - genuine 86
Faith - justification by (see Justification)
Faith - reckoned 20
Faith - righteousness by 3,8,9,19,24,27,29,30,32,
........33,36,41-44,48,52,53,59,67-71,79,81,83,84,87,107,111
Faith - the just shall live by 18,82
Faith - virtue in 92,95
Faithful ones 91
Fasting 78
Fear - from within and without 34,114
Findlay, G.G. 72
Formalism 32,33,37,62,71,72,78,104
Formalism - drifting into 32
Forms - external 32,78,104
G
Gems of truth 8
General conference 9,27,39,42,45
Gentiles 17,23
Gilboa 47,78
Glory - immortal 91
God - curse of born by Jesus 39
God - forbearance of 19,22

TOPICAL INDEX (Cont'd)

G (Cont'd)   **Page**
God - name hallowed 24
God - offended 22,119
God - peace with 23,60,62,71,97
God - plenitude of 21
God - profered help of 31
God - will of..36,75,104
God - character - possessed by man 24,77,88,94,95
Godliness - practical 33,74,75
Godliness - true 34,46,104,112
Gospel - truths of 37,73
Grace 19,22,24,60,61,70,72,73,75,77,78,84,89,94,97,
...............................102,104,105,108,112,115,119,129
Grace - oil of 77,102
Guilt - cancelled 19,61,62
H
Heart - new 88
Heart - thine 24
Heaven 2,10,24,29,33,35,37,39,40,46,49-52,54,55,60,
...............69,75,78,79,83,85-89,93,94,102-104,107,113,116,
....117,119,121-124,128
Holy Ghost 72,108,119
Holy Spirit 56,57,62,69,73,75,83,106,111,113,118,
.... 120,122,123,125,127-130
Hope 20,21,24,27,34,35,37,43,44,62,75,86,87,94,97
I
Idols 36,72,112
Instruction 9,10,31,34,35,39,40,53,67,68,71,97
Iowa 8
J
Jacob 47,50,117
Jeremiah 31
Jesus - commander of angels 40
Jesus - death - astonishment to universe 39

TOPICAL INDEX (Cont'd)

J (Cont'd)   **Page**

Jesus - door to door 2,102
Jesus - faith of 60,61
Jesus - iniquity - hated 16,22
Jesus - knocking 38
Jesus - lowliness 39,40
Jesus - many had lost sight of 28
Jesus - meekness 39,40
Jesus - nature - holy 40,111
Jesus - nature - more exalted 40
Jesus - nature - pure 40,111
Jesus - ransom paid 85,87
Jesus - self denial 39
Judah - kingdom of 31
Justice 68,85,87,108
Justification by faith 8,44,51,59,60-62,67,69,70,79,
....80,81,92
Justified 18-20,22,23,60,62,71,86,87,92,97,108

L

Laodicea 45,80,110,125
Law 18,19,21-24,35,37-39,46-48,56,59,60,62,
.....................68,75,82,85-87,90,94,103,107-109,126,129
Law - accepted 19
Law - condemnation of 21,59,62
Law - curse of 86
Law - demands of 21,22,86,107
Law - works of 23,87
Leaven 73,124,129
Lesson 9,61,68,74,77,106,108,119,126
Life - former manner of 16
Light - precious 45,83
Light - refusing 51
Lot 17
Love - first lost 110,118,122,125

TOPICAL INDEX (Cont'd)

L (Cont'd)   **Page**
Love - unparalleled 56,84,126,129
Luther, Martin 81,82
M
Man - mortal 26
Manifestations - important 58
Merchantman - heavenly 2,96,102
Merit . 22,23,28,47,52,70,75,86,92,93,95,96,97,107,108,124
Message - awakening 27
Message - precious 27,28,45
Message - preparatory 31,39,79
Message - startling 37
Message - third angel's 28,29,49,50,53-62,67,79,80,
....83,109,125
Message - third angel's - heavenly endorsement 29
Message - third angel's - righteousness by faith 59-62,80
Message - third angel's - with loud voice 28,29,55
Message - third angel's - work - soul cleansing 27,29,46,
.... 60,74,87
Mind - unilluminated 22
Minister 8,27,32,39,40,46,47,50,51,73,82,83,103,
....115,116,120
Ministerial Association 8
Minneapolis 9,27,29,32,39,42-44,53,58,59,67
Moses - law of 35
Mount of Olives 33
Movement - reformatory 122,123
N
Nature - human 16,17,35,39,86,88
Need - greatest and most urgent 34
New Testament 18,127
New teaching 42
Noah 17
Nothingness - man's own 92

TOPICAL INDEX (Cont'd)

O   **Page**

Obedience - perfect 22,95-97,108

Obligation 8

Opinions - differences of among leaders 42

Opposition - decided   43

Orthodoxy - true 72

P

Pardon 22,23,37,53,56,58,61,85-87,92,94,95,98,101,
....102,107-109,126,129

Paul 17-20,22,23,33,61,72

Pentecost 123,128

Perdition 90

Peril 31,33,37,51,56,57,71,72,110,118,124,125

Perplexity 42,59,67

Pharisee 74,104,106

Pierson..66

Piety 72-74,78

Poverty - soul 105

Power 15,18,24,28,33-36,38,43,45,46,51,52,54-57,61,
..............67,72,74,75,77-81,83,88,89,91-95,97,101-106,109,
.... 113-116,119-123,126,128

Power - broken 51,52

Power - in prayer 73

Power - reservoir of 85

Power - supernatural to sinner 52,80,81,94,95,97

Prayer - Lord's 24

Prominence - message great 27

Propitiation 19,22

Providence of God 9,53

Provision - God's 34

Purity 38,88,101,104

R

Rain - early 57,128

Rain - latter 55,57,128

TOPICAL INDEX (Cont'd)

R (Cont'd)	**Page**
Reconversion	119
Redeemed	11,69,91
Redeemer	2,15,22,37,46,53,56,58,61,69,71,90,101,103
Redemption	22,36,37,40,68,70,85,96,101,106,108
Religion - Christless	76
Religion - profession of	35
Remnant church	8,10,31,42,55,110
Restoration	7,46,85,86,90
Revival	34,40,45,46,112,113,118,120,122
Righteousness - awake to	14,16
Righteousness - blessing of	18
Righteousness - everlasting	16
Righteousness - exalt His	48
Righteousness - filthy rags	46,81,93
Righteousness - imputeth	20
Righteousness - in all His ways	16,20
Righteousness - like the great mountains	16
Righteousness - nature of	16
Righteousness - obtained by	15,18
Righteousness - personal relation to	16
Righteousness - source of	15,16
Righteousness - way of	9,20,23
Righteousness by faith - an experience	24,62,70,71,74
Righteousness by faith - is new birth	24
Righteousness by faith - is regeneration	24
Righteousness by faith - is transaction	18,19,21-24,80,97
Righteousness by faith - not theory	24,70
Righteousness of Christ - imputed	9,21,22,35,36,70, 79,87,88,96,127
Righteousness of Christ - pearl	70,96,97
Righteousness - robe of Christ's	26
S	
Salt	71,73,76,129

TOPICAL INDEX (Cont'd)

S (Cont'd)

Page

Sanctuary 26,69,73,74,77,113,116
Sardis 121
Saviour - sacrifice 19,22,28,37,44,56,68,78,
......................................85-88,93,101,108,109,128,129
Schaff, Dr. Philip 94
Scriptural authority 9
Security - way of 37
Service - religious 33,37
Sin - deliverance from 19,21,69,94
Sin - knowledge of 18,19
Sin - no relish for 90,92
Sin - remission of 19,22,128
Sin - repudiation of 71
Sin - righteousness opposite of 16,71
Sinner - hopeless 20,94,97
Solution 22
Spirit of prophecy 8-10,27,32,33,43,53-55,67-69,71,
....72,80,84,95
Spiritual blindness 50,51,111
Spiritual drought 111
Spiritual feebleness 120
Spiritual gifts 120
Spiritual lethargy 110
Spiritual paralysis 110
Spiritual slumber 110,125
Spirituality dying 33,48,49
Stupor 110,125
Surety - faith in 28

T

Temptation - hour of 54
Test - time of 53,56,125
Time - fearful and solemn 35,116
Times - apostolic 18

143

TOPICAL INDEX (Cont'd)

T (Cont'd)   **Page**

True way 36,37

Truth 8,9,15,16,19,23,29,37,38,39-47,49,50-52,59,
.... 62,67,68-71,73,74,75,77,79-84,89,93,96,97,
.... 107,109,111,114,116,118,119,121,123,124-127

Truth - framework of 84

Truth - present 45,82,106,116

Truth - scriptures of 16,124

U

Unacquainted 9

V

Verity - third angel's message 59-61

Virgins - five foolish 77

W

Waiting one, the 3

Wandered 9

Wheels within the wheels 33

White, E.G. 2,8,11,45,59

Word of God 5,9,15,16,32,45,69,123,127,129

Z

Zacharias 17

Zeal 38,47,76,80,125